Claudio and Fabrizio Porrozzi

# SUPERBIKE

THE OFFICIAL BOOK
2009-2010

GIORGIO NADA EDITORE

**Giorgio Nada Editore Srl**

**Editorial Coordination**
Leonardo Acerbi

**Based on an idea by**
Claudio Porrozzi

**Photo Editor**
Fabrizio Porrozzi

**Art director**
Cinzia Giuriolo

**Editing**
Diana Calarco

**Photographs**
Fabrizio Porrozzi
TL Studio: M. Teresa Degrandi - Luca Burato
Picture pag. 79 by Roger Lohrer

© 2009 Giorgio Nada Editore, Vimodrone (Milano) - Italy

**ALL RIGHTS RESERVED**
*All rights reserved. Apart from any fair dealing for the purpose of private study, research, criticism or review, no part of this publication may be reproduced, stored in a retrieval system, or transmitted, by any means, electronic, electrical, chemical, mechanical, optical photocopying, recording or otherwise, without prior written permission.
All enquiries should be addressed to the publisher:*

**Giorgio Nada Editore**
Via Claudio Treves, 15/17
I – 20090 VIMODRONE - MI - ITALY
Tel. +39 02 27301126
Fax +39 02 27301454
E-mail: info@giorgionadaeditore.it
http://www.giorgionadaeditore.it

*The catalogue of Giorgio Nada Editore publications is available on request at the above address.*

**Distributed by:**
Giunti Editore Spa
via Bolognese 165
I – 50139 FIRENZE
www.giunti.it

Superbike 2009-2010. The Official Book
ISBN: 978-88-7911-468-4

| | | |
|---|---|---|
| | That's Superbike | 06 |
| Claudio Porrozzi | WSBK Champion | 12 |
| | WSBK Riders | 18 |
| | Teams | 24 |
| | WSBK Races | 40 |
| Julian Thomas | Gardner | 96 |
| Gordon Ritchie | Technology | 100 |
| | Tyres | 130 |
| Gordon Ritchie | WSS Champion | 136 |
| | WSS Riders | 142 |
| | WSS Races | 146 |
| Federico Porrozzi | STK 1000 Champion | 176 |
| | STK 1000 Riders | 180 |
| Federico Porrozzi | STK 600 Champion | 186 |
| | STK 600 Riders | 192 |

# Summary

The FIM Superbike and Supersport World Championships and the Superstock FIM Cup have had increasing success throughout recent years. We just have witnessed an extraordinary 2009 season in which the Superbike Championship was decided at the very last race, and the Champion received his crown by just a handful of points ahead of his main contender. It was definitely one of the most interesting and successful seasons since the Series was created in 1988. This shows how much progress and development has been made year after year.

The production-based motorcycles from the manufacturers are racing on circuits and giving us a fantastic sporting show, underlining the high level and success of this competition. This can be linked directly with the success of this type of motorcycle in many world markets. And this year with two more manufacturers – and also new riders - taking part in the Championship it has become even more attractive.

The Supersport Championship season has also been very exciting, with great racing in all rounds, and the Superstock FIM Cup has given us a fantastic show with young riders who will be the Champions of tomorrow, already providing us with great competition and an astonishing level in riding and skill.

I would first like to greet the 2009 Champions: Ben Spies, Cal Crutchlow and Xavier Siméon – and then all the persons involved in the Superbike and Supersport World Championships and Superstock FIM Cup, our partner Infront Motor Sports, the National Federations, the organisers, and all the riders and teams, the media and, of course, the spectators who are making Superbike a top series in our sport.

Vito Ippolito
FIM President

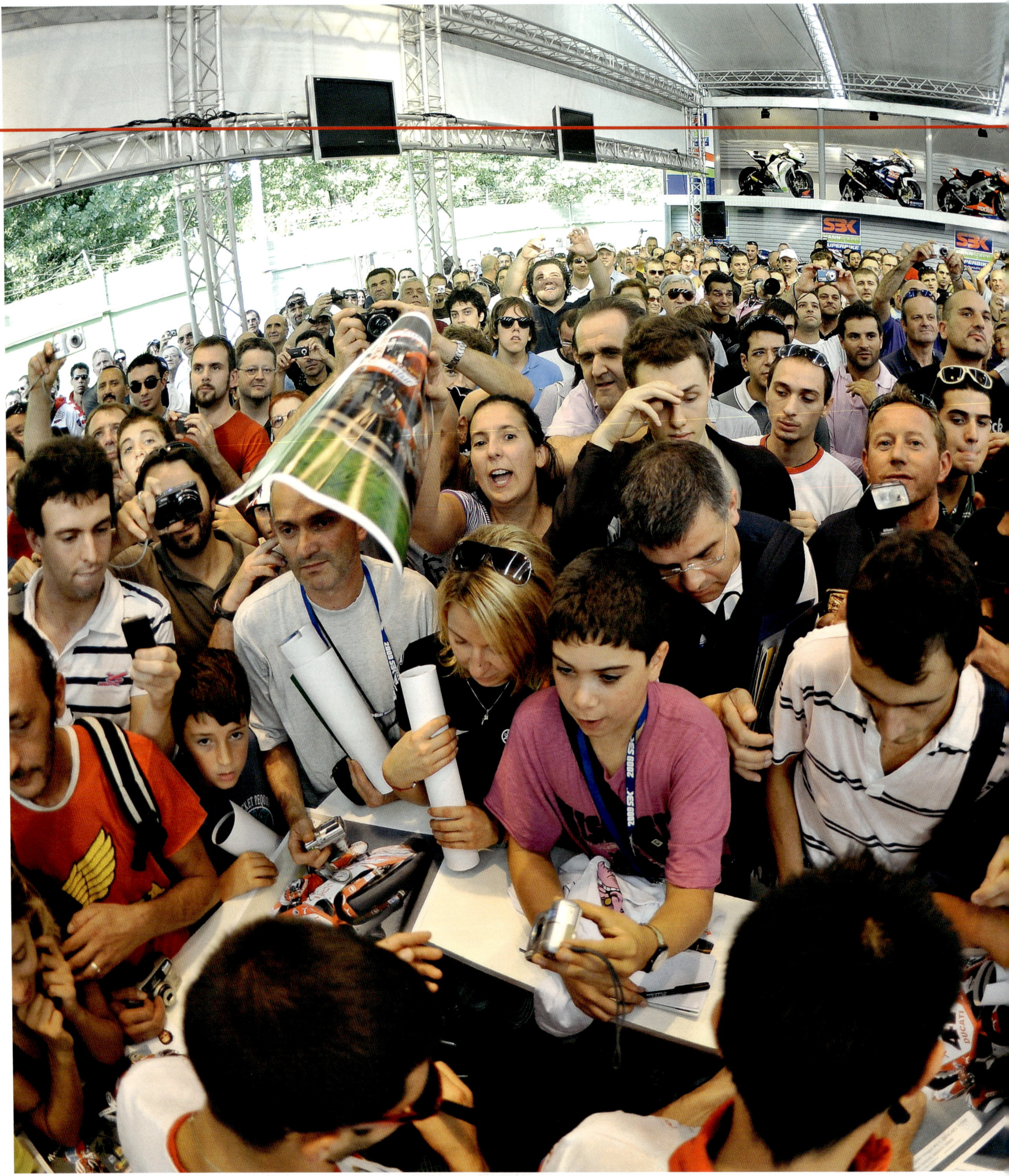
SBK
2008 SBK
DUCATI

## WSBK Championship
# That's Superbike

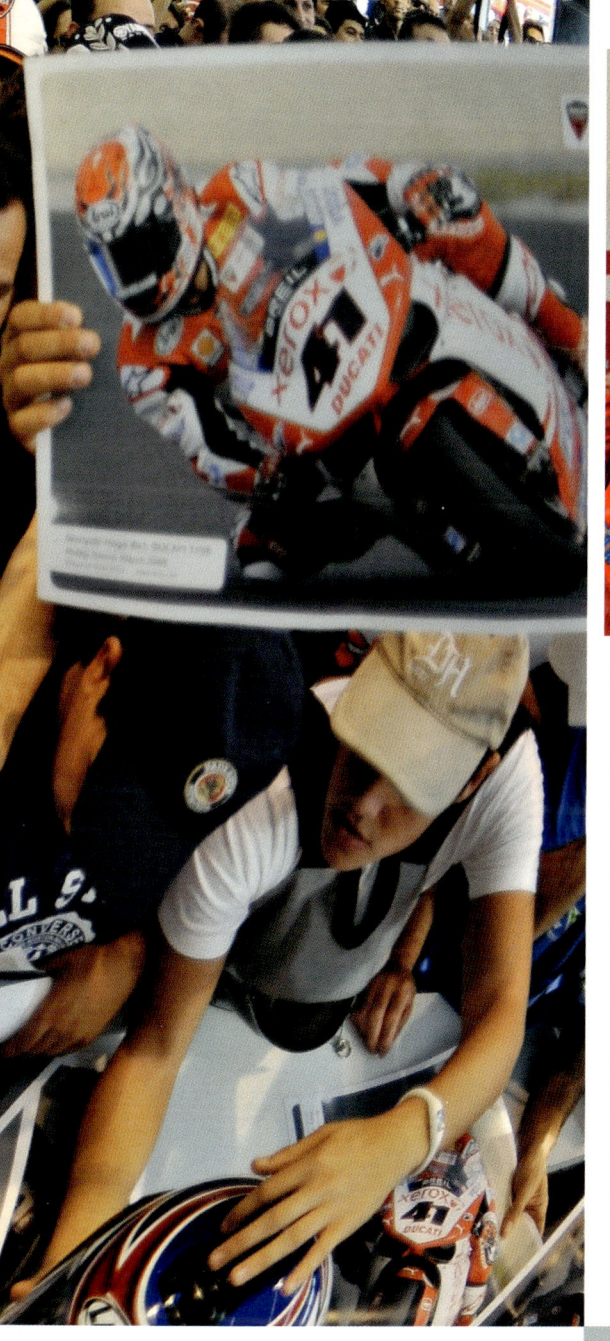

What exactly is Superbike? It's difficult to give a brief description because the production-based world championship series is a combination of essential elements that join together in 14 splendid appointments in four continents around the world.

First of all there are the bikes, and with seven manufacturers present, these represent a sort of technical and entrepreneurial elite from the world of two wheels.

Then there are the riders, from all over the world, with racing 'veterans' shaping up against youngsters who are bursting with talent and anxious to emerge in the two-race format rounds.

Let's not forget the other essential personnel; the engineers and mechanics who design, prepare and run the bikes with which their riders attempt to win races.

And finally the spectators, traditionally made up of true fans and experts who appreciate the philosophy of the world championship and are familiar with every little detail. And 'their' championship rewards them with access to the Paddock and the garages where they can meet their idols and see the bikes close up.

This, and much more, is Superbike!

# WSBK Championship

*The spectators are one of the fundamental elements of the Superbike World Championship, which bases a large part of its philosophy on contact with the fans, generally some of the most competent in the world of bike racing.*

# WSBK Championship

≡ *One of the biggest and best reasons to follow Superbike is the access to the Paddock, where fans have a chance to meet the riders who willingly make themselves available for the general public.*

To become 2009 champion (in the photo, the four class winners) the riders had to take part in 14 rounds around the world, all broadcast on TV.

WSBK Championship

# WSBK Champion
# Ben Spies

Accustomed as we were to the warmth and friendliness of Troy Bayliss, it seems a bit strange to meet a rider like Ben Spies, who has a completely different character to the Australian.

This does not mean that the American is disagreeable or anything like that, but he's just a bit reserved and this is a very particular characteristic for a rider, especially a Superbike rider. Unfortunately it is this category that Spies will immediately abandon because in 2010 he will be switching to MotoGP to race with Yamaha once again. So that means that Spies's only World Superbike championship season will not go unobserved!

He arrived at the end of the 2008 season, when the Yamaha management found themselves in the not easy situation of having to replace Noriyuki Haga, who had moved to Ducati. Rather than look for someone already within Superbike, Kleinkoerkamp and Meregalli opted to search elsewhere and their attention immediately fell on Ben Spies, a young American who had won three AMA Superbike titles in the USA.

At 24 years of age, Spies had considerable experience in America where he had to shape up against a figure of the caliber of Mat Mladin, an Australian with a long and experienced history who had found his second coming in the USA series.

Considering that the two were team-mates in Suzuki, Ben's form was truly impressive but in the three MotoGP races in which he took part he didn't stand out too much. As a replacement for the injured Capirossi in the 2008 British GP, he finished 14th, a result that was followed by 8th place at Laguna Seca and 6th place at Indianapolis, all three races on a Suzuki.

Born on July 11th, 1984 in Memphis, Tennessee, Spies started to score results in road racing in 2000, when he finished in ninth place in the AMA Superstock championship and then third the following year in Superstock 750. In his three years in Supersport the best was 2004 when he finished fourth, a result that earned him a place in Superbike. After finishing second in 2005, Ben then won the AMA title the next three years on the run. He is also the rider who set the record of seven successive wins in one season (2008) of AMA Superbike racing.

His debut in the world championship was surrounded by high expectations, especially af-

19
PARTS EUROPE
AKRAPOVIČ
FIMER
sterilgarda
alimenti
domino
BM GROUP
YAMAHA
Sponsor del Benessere
YAMALUBE
FERODO
HJC

# WSBK Champion

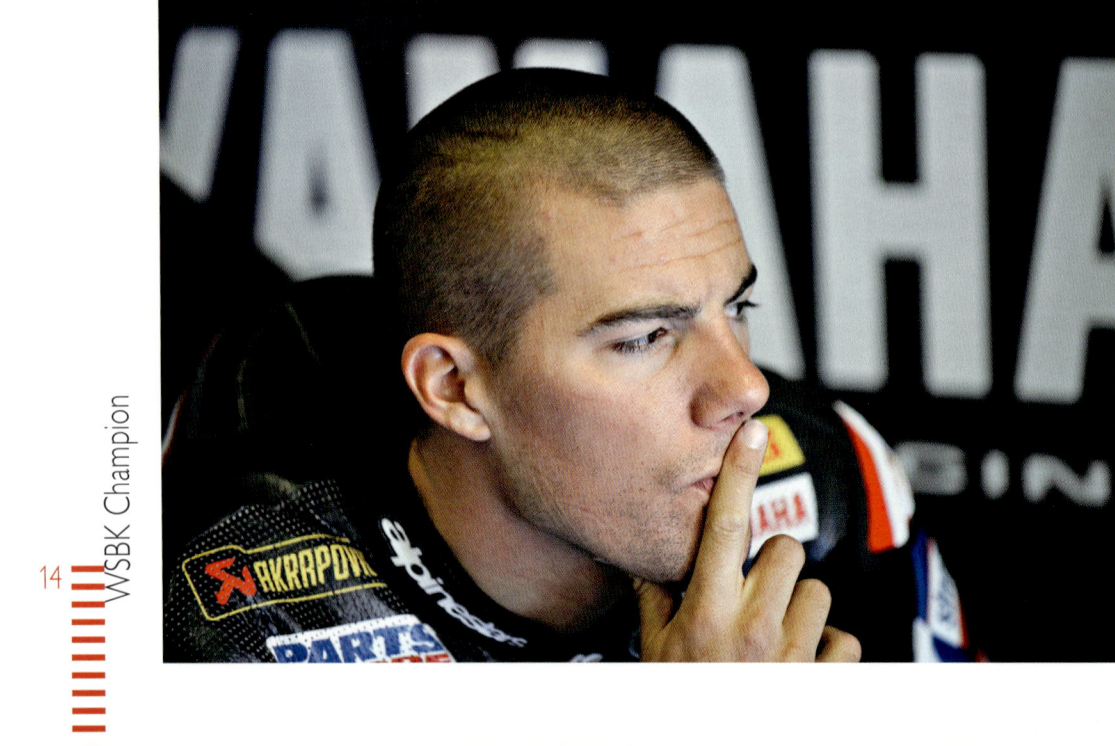

ter winter testing when the American had impressed for his determination and his ability to rapidly learn the tracks.

It wasn't much of a surprise therefore to see him on pole position at Phillip Island for the opening round and take his first win, again in Australia. From then on it was a season that went spiralling upwards, starting with a double win at Losail (Qatar). Not even a crash at Valencia, nor the fuel running out at Monza, nor being taken out by Fabrizio at Brno could halt his march towards the title.

Like almost all American riders Spies showed enormous determination and above all, never gave up when the points gap to the top appeared to be overwhelming. He began the recovery in the second half of the season and was crowned champion on his debut, just like another Texan, Doug Polen, in 1991 with Ducati. But his real strength lay in the psychological attack on his adversaries who were always waiting for him to produce the goods both in Superpole (where he scored 11 wins) and in the races, where his acceleration was a prelude to him going on to win (and this he did 14 times). In the post-race interviews Ben would appear rather amazed that people were asking him about his exceptional performances, as if they

*Ben Spies never abandoned his spectacular and characteristic 'elbows-out' riding style throughout his 14 race wins.*

## WSBK Champion

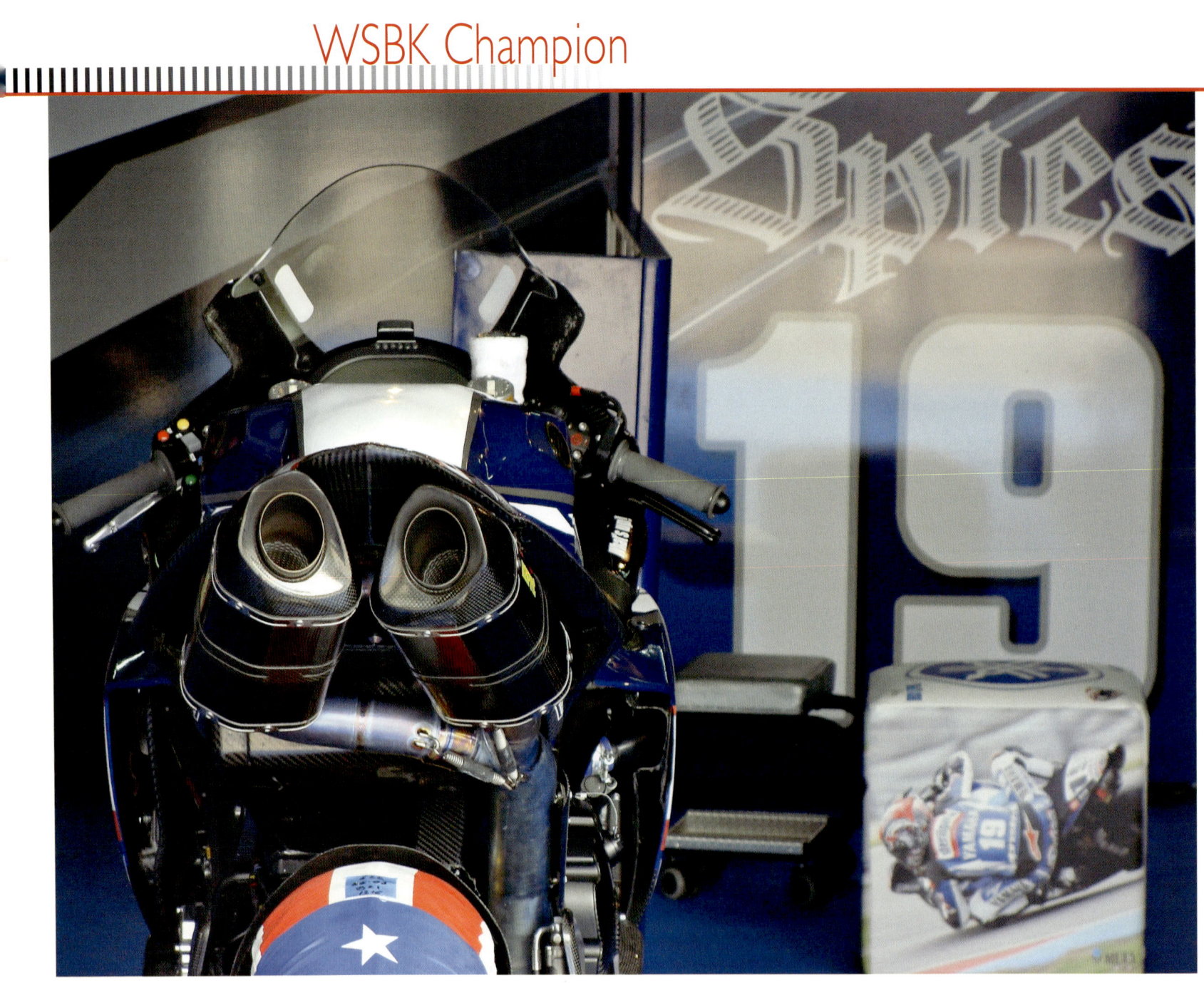

*The feeling between Spies and his team was an excellent one in the American's rookie WSB season, in which he took 11 Superpoles.*

were (for him at least) normal administration. The always courteous and timidly smiling American was already maybe thinking of his return to Lake Como where he lived in between races and when he wasn't in America. Because Spies is a man who loves a life of peace and quiet, interspersed with fishing and numerous cycling sessions, staying with his mum who followed him throughout the season.

But he doesn't disdain the company of his fellow riders either, and one of those whom he struck up a friendship with was his chief rival Haga, and they often organized a barbecue together.

Now a new phase of his career is about to begin for Spies, but the American will certainly remain in the hearts of many and in particular in Superbike history for many years to come.

WSBK Champion

# WSBK Riders

The battle for the 2009 Superbike World Championship title only concluded, as we all saw, at the final round when Ben Spies won race 1 and finished fifth in race 2 to defeat Noriyuki Haga. It was one of the most exciting championships ever held with a constant series of surprises and upsets that left the battle uncertain right down to the last round.

After six rounds the championship appeared to be firmly in the grasp of Haga but the Japanese rider once again had to come to terms with what appears to be his destiny: finishing runner-up (for the third time in his career). This year Nori seemed to have decided to break this jinx by switching from Yamaha, with whom he had virtually raced for ever, to Ducati – the bike on which he made his WSB debut in 1994 – but this change was all for nothing. The 34 year-old from Nagoya, who finished runner-up in 2000 and 2007, had 88 points advantage over his chief rival for the title, Ben Spies, by the mid-season at Kyalami. The situation underwent a radical change immediately after with a dominant double win by Spies at Miller Motorsports Park in Salt Lake City. It then took a turn for the worse at Donington, when Nori finished third in race 1 and crashed out badly in race 2. At Brno Haga's condition was not 100% and in the subsequent races the Japanese rider never appeared to be his usual aggressive self. He took eight wins, which took his overall total to 41 out of 286 races.

Finally free of the 'cumbersome' presence of Troy Bayliss, Italian Michel Fabrizio seemed to have found a new dimension in winter testing. Then in the opening round the first and second place of his team-mate was an eye-opener and his disastrous races in Qatar did the rest. But the Rome rider has changed and is maturing all the time, so then at Valencia with two podiums he found his self-confidence again. Fabrizio scored three wins, the first at Monza, where he was gifted victory by Spies's Yamaha running out of fuel, then a deserved victory at Imola in front of Haga and the season closer at Portimao.

Max Biaggi had a lot of courage to take on the task of making the Aprilia RSV4 competitive and he was rewarded by the win at Brno. The 38 year-old Italian still wants to show everyone that he is a champion, and even though sometimes he appeared to be just a little too calculating, he succeeded in the intent by taking fourth overall, with eight podiums in total. The rapport between the Rome man and Aprilia is a long-standing one and the presence of the team led by Giovanni Sandi guarantees a good feeling and technical competence. The 2009 season was born from this and it can be seen as a success,

*Nori Haga was the points leader for most of the season but a crash at Donington brought an end to his run of positive results and the second half of the season became much more difficult; right down to the championship decider in Portugal, which saw Haga take the runner-up slot.*

WSBK Riders

WSBK Riders

## WSBK Riders

especially in comparison with other seasoned riders and illustrious debutants.
Britain has been in search of a valid replacement for 2007 WSB champion James Toseland and this year they found at least two. It will be interesting to see how they shape up against the former MotoGP rider next year. The most impressive was Jonathan Rea, 22 years old from Ballymena, Northern Ireland, yet another Ten Kate discovery. In his first full Superbike season he took two wins at Misano and Nurburgring, proving to have a determination that sometimes took him over the limit. As soon as he learns how to administer his undeniable talent, he will be a tough rival for everyone. The second British rider was Leon Haslam, who at 26 years of age is only slightly more expert than Rea. Leon is no longer known as the son of Rocket Ron but has become a competitive rider in his own right. He has yet to step onto the top of the podium but was always up amongst the front runners despite the financial problems afflicting his Stiggy Racing team. Two second places at Assen and Donington were his best results.
And we remain in Britian to have a look at the season of Shane Byrne, who despite his 33 years of age is still able to produce some superb races. With the Ducati of the Marco Borciani-run Sterilgarda team Byrne was always up at the front and

*Two riders in particular had a very special rivalry, both having been born in the Italian capital, Rome. Michel Fabrizio (84) is improving race by race and in 2010 could be a real contender for the title, while Max Biaggi (above), following a learning season with the RSV4, will also be aiming for the top slot next year.*

# WSBK Riders

in the end he finished eighth, just ahead of Tom Sykes. The former BSB man lost his way a bit in the second half of the season and most certainly lost out in the confrontation between him and his fellow rookie, team-mate Ben Spies, both of whom were at their first experiences with the Yamaha R1.

Carlos Checa continues to be one of the most popular riders around and on the Ten Kate Honda the Spaniard picked up seventh place overall (a result that helps him keep his favourite number 7 next season). Two second places at Miller and Brno were his best results, which came after early season difficulties had been resolved by the team's switch to Ohlins suspension, but unlike 2008 this year he didn't win any races.

The top 10 is concluded with a young rider who comes from an emerging nation, the Czech Republic, where Jakub Smrz was born in 1983 at Ceské Budejovice. Smrz was on the Guandalini private Ducati and he managed to set pole position at Misano, where the advice from his team manager Pierfrancesco Chili came in useful, and to step onto the final podium slot at Assen. Jakub was always fast but has to learn how to stay with the leading group and not to make any errors.

We have just had a look at four of the manufacturers (Yamaha, Ducati, Aprilia and Honda) out of the seven officially present in the 2009 FIM Superbike World Championship. The other three were unfortunately unable to replicate that sort of winning form, starting with Suzuki, who after the incident to Max Neukirchner were unable to go any higher than fifth place in the Manufacturers' standings (and 12th with Yukio Kagayama in the Riders' classification).

A lot of expectation surrounded BMW's debut, especially in view of the German manufacturer's reputation and notable technological potential. Unfortunately they found the going tough in their first year and despite the efforts of Corser and Xaus, the best result for the team was a fifth place for the Australian at Brno, although it must be said that considerable progress was made in the second part of the year.

The season was even less positive for the Kawasaki World Superbike Racing Team, which despite switching to the British PBM outfit was unable to make much of an impression in the results and the final standings. Kawasaki's best result was a seventh place for substitute rider Hacking at Miller.

Jonathan Rea (65) was, together with Spies, the surprise of the season; he won two races and was always fast. Leon Haslam (91) also had a positive season, the British rider often riding over the problems, while Carlos Checa (7) was competitive on occasions on the Ten Kate Honda CBR1000RR.

WSBK Riders

Honda Racing
Honda Racing
YAMAHA
YAMAHA
ACTROS
SBK
SUPERBIKE WORLD CHAMPIONSHIP

# WSBK Championship Teams

**H**ow often have we heard people speak about the importance of the rider and the machine when it comes down to performance? There are a number of different views on this issue and the percentage given to each component varies according to the time and the championship. It doesn't seem to be common however to refer to a third important component in bike racing: the team. And this is rather curious because the factors that contribute to a result or a win should clearly include the organization, the management and the technical ability of the personnel who work on the bike.

A team can come about for a variety of reasons: the strategic choice of a company that wants to race with its own bike, the desire of an entrepreneur who is looking for a professional outlet in motor sport or plain and simple passion.

The latter is the least common because the technical level in Superbike is so high that it requires a substantial commitment for which unfortunately passion for bikes and motor sport in general is not sufficient. But in each one of the teams that take part in the production-based world championship emotional involvement in the world of motorbikes is fundamental, and just as decisive as the high technical and professional level on display.

In this chapter we would like to present, through a series of images, all the teams that took part in the 2009 Superbike World Championship, both the factory teams and the private squads. It aims to be partial recognition for all those people who are hard at work before the start lights go off and after the chequered flag has been waved. It also shows how the different teams shaped up in the paddock and the pit garages around the world and throughout the season. It's curious to see the choice of colours, the way the tools are laid out and used, and the faces of the people involved. But there is only one common denominator: the bike is the true protagonist.

# Teams

Ducati won the Manufacturers' title and its two riders, Nori Haga and Michel Fabrizio took second and third place in the Riders' championship with 11 wins.

After years of trying Yamaha succeeded in winning the Riders' championship with American Ben Spies, who was flanked by Britain's Tom Sykes. The Japanese manufacturer won 14 races, all with Spies.

*For several years now the Dutch Ten Kate Honda team has been one of the protagonists of World Superbike (its last title came in 2007 with Toseland) and with this year's riders (Jonathan Rea and Carlos Checa), it picked up two wins.*

# Teams

*The real surprise of the 2009 season was Aprilia, whose riders were Max Biaggi and Shinya Nakano, then replaced by Leon Camier. The Italian took the RSV4 to victory at Brno.*

# Teams

It was a difficult season for the Stiggy Racing Team which entered two Honda CBR1000RR for Leon Haslam (in the photo) and John Hopkins. The British rider managed to finish sixth overall in the championship.

It was a tough season for everyone but the Suzuki Alstare team was unlucky to lose Max Neukirchner in a crash at Monza. Neither Yukio Kagayama nor the other riders were able to take the GSX-R1000 to the top.

Teams

There was much expectation surrounding the debut of BMW and on a few occasions the bike showed glimpses of its potential in the hands of Troy Corser and Ruben Xaus. The team made a major effort on a technological and financial level but this investment was not rewarded by the results, which will certainly arrive in the future.

# Teams

*Kawasaki lined up at the start of the season with high hopes following a radical change of its team outfit and structure. Unfortunately, maybe due to its scarce experience in the world championship, the PBM team was unable to obtain many good results. Broc Parkes and Makoto Tamada were the riders for the British-based team.*

# Teams

≡ *Ducati also allows its private teams to be competitive, on condition that they are well-organized structures like the Marco Borciani-run Sterilgarda team (above, Shane Byrne) or Guandalini Ducati (below).*

≡ *The Pedercini Kawasaki team and its riders Luca Scassa and David Salom (above) made a big effort and were full of determination. A good dose of passion and considerable technical competence were the hallmarks of the Althea Honda team, who didn't have much luck in its choice of riders.*

≡ *Another competitive Ducati team was DFX Corse, but its rider Regis Laconi (above) was sidelined by a serious crash. The rookie Squadra Corse Italia team on the other hand opted for a Honda with its rider Vittorio Iannuzzo.*

# Teams

≡ GMT94 has considerable experience in Endurance but has also been a regular presence in Superbike over the years. It was a tough debut instead for the Austrian TKR team, which chose a Suzuki for its first year in World Superbike.

# WSBK Championship

# SUPERBIKE RACES

# (23.02) Phillip Island (AUS)

Phillip Island saw the introduction of the new Superpole formula, which was met with a mixed response. One rider in favour was Ben Spies, who was clearly used to setting the pole position.

The American appeared to be surprised by the questions from journalists after he had demolished the record of a track he had never seen before, lowering it by four-tenths to 1 minute 31.069 seconds. Alongside Spies on the front row could be found Max Biaggi with the Aprilia RSV4 making its Superbike championship debut. Jonathan Rea, the young British rider in the Hannspree Ten Kate Honda team, also notched up a superb third after running at the top for much of the session. The front row was completed by privateer Jakub Smrz (Ducati Guandalini), while Michel Fabrizio, after setting a good time in the second run, was slowed by a defective tyre in the decisive third stage.

Things went worse for Haga, who was excluded from the final session and would start from row 4. BMW made a strategic error that highlighted their relative lack of experience in bike racing: they decided to use race tyres in the first stage, keeping the regulation two soft ones for the final two runs, but the result was that Troy Corser and Ruben Xaus started from row 5!

## RACE 1

The race was declared 'wet' a few minutes before the start. Rea took the lead and tried to pull away but on lap 3 Haga (Ducati Xerox) took control followed by Laconi (Ducati DFX). Biaggi made a great start from the front row but already by lap 2 he was down to ninth, while poleman Spies (Yamaha) went on the grass and returned to the track in last place.

Neukirchner (Suzuki) started well and with a sequence of quick laps moved into third, then second and then into the lead on the ninth of the 22 laps. But Haga was right there controlling the German until lap 18 when he retook the lead.

The Suzuki man stayed on Haga's exhausts and on the final lap managed to slipstream past once again, but Haga was a tough nut to crack and he forced Max into making

xerox
41
DUCATI
BREIL
MILANO
ADVANCE
valsir
Arai
HELMET
NKI41.COM

WSBK Races

# WSBK Championship

an error, which gave him the opportunity to win the first race of the season. Kagayama completed the podium with the other Suzuki. Michel Fabrizio, who finished third here last year, had a good run from row 2, recovering from a bad start to eventually finish fourth, while a determined Troy Corser took the BMW S1000 RR to eighth. Aprilia's hopes were in part dashed as Biaggi hovered constantly around tenth place to finish eleventh, while Nakano could only notch up fifteenth.

## RACE 2

After his first experience of Phillip Island in race 1, Spies led for much of the second encounter, holding off the attacks from Haga who settled for the runner-up slot following his earlier win.

The man to watch however was Biaggi on the brand-new Aprilia RSV4. The Italian grabbed the lead from the start and managed to stay on the same pace as Haga and Spies. But in the second half of the race he lost contact with his two rivals and ended up fighting for third with Fabrizio (Ducati Xerox), Haslam (Stiggy Racing Honda) and Laconi. Unfortunately he ended up on the grass in an effort to stay with the others and could only finish fifteenth.

Third place went to privateer Haslam, whose Swedish Stiggy team was rivalling the established Ten Kate outfit as top Honda squad. The British rider took Fabrizio on the final lap, immediately followed by Laconi with the Ducati DFX machine. BMW again made progress with Ruben Xaus this time taking eleventh place ahead of the second Aprilia of Nakano.

*Under the watchful eyes of Troy Bayliss the 2009 Superbike World Championship got underway with seven manufacturer teams present. The opening round saw the wins go to Haga (41) and Spies (19), while Max Neukirchner (75) also went well.*

| | | | Race 1 |
|---|---|---|---|
| 1° | N. Haga | (JPN - Ducati) | 34'22"631 |
| | | | 170,677 km/h |
| 2° | M. Neukirchner | (GER - Suzuki) | + 0"032 |
| 3° | Y. Kagayama | (JPN - Suzuki) | + 5"347 |
| 4° | M. Fabrizio | (ITA - Ducati) | + 6"587 |
| 5° | J. Rea | (GBR - Honda) | + 8"491 |

| | | | Race 2 |
|---|---|---|---|
| 1° | B. Spies | (USA - Yamaha) | 34'20"457 |
| | | | 170,857 km/h |
| 2° | N. Haga | (JPN - Ducati) | + 1"286 |
| 3° | L. Haslam | (GBR - Honda) | + 4"213 |
| 4° | R. Laconi | (FRA - Ducati) | + 4"490 |
| 5° | M. Fabrizio | (ITA - Ducati) | + 6"045 |

WSBK Races

44

# Losail (QATAR) (14.03)

| Race 1 | | | |
|---|---|---|---|
| 1° | B. Spies | (USA - Yamaha) | 36'06"304 |
| | | | 160,930 km/h |
| 2° | N. Haga | (JPN - Ducati) | + 1"893 |
| 3° | M. Biaggi | (ITA - Aprilia) | + 2'168 |
| 4° | S. Nakano | (JPN - Aprilia) | + 12"061 |
| 5° | C. Checa | (ESP - Honda) | + 12"597 |

| Race 2 | | | |
|---|---|---|---|
| 1° | B. Spies | (USA - Yamaha) | 36'02"126 |
| | | | 161,241 km/h |
| 2° | N. Haga | (JPN - Ducati) | + 1"274 |
| 3° | M. Biaggi | (ITA - Aprilia) | + 1'622 |
| 4° | R. Kiyonari | (JPN - Honda) | + 1"845 |
| 5° | T. Sykes | (GBR - Yamaha) | + 5"117 |

*Ben Spies burst onto the WSB scene with his first double win of the season on his second outing with the factory Yamaha in Qatar.*

Yamaha and Ben Spies were on top of their game in qualifying, with the American holding off Max Biaggi to clinch the Superpole in the final session. Czech rider Jakub Smrz was the best of the Ducatis, his private Guandalini machine qualifying ahead of the factory bikes. The first Xerox machine, that of Haga, was also on the front row, while Biaggi continued to improve the feeling with his Aprilia to end up fourth.

**RACE 1**

Biaggi got the best start to lead by a few metres from Haga, Smrz, Spies, Nakano (Aprilia) and Laconi (DFX Ducati), while Corser was lying in eighth place. On lap 5 Haga tried to pass Biaggi, while Spies was closing after seeing off Smrz and Nakano.

Checa (Honda) was sixth and Fabrizio seventh after a poor start, but the Italian crashed on lap 8 while lapping at the same pace as the leaders. Neukirchner also crashed twice and was out of the race. On lap 8 Smrz did the same and was unable to restart, while the leading trio were almost four seconds ahead of Nakano and six ahead of Checa.

Ben Spies controlled the situation from the back of the leading group until a third of the way before the end when he first passed Haga and then Biaggi to head for the win. Haga also passed Biaggi but the Italian forced his way past again: they were already distanced from Spies by half-a-second and were holding each other up while Spies got away.

The American was lapping constantly at under the two minute mark and he went on to take his second win of the year by almost two seconds from Haga and Biaggi.

The others were some way behind, the best being Nakano at over 12 seconds, which just about sums up the pace of the leading trio. The Japanese rider was followed home by Checa and Byrne.

**RACE 2**

There was nothing that could be done about Ben Spies either in race 2 and even Haga and Biaggi didn't force the pace when they realized that they couldn't keep up with the American. Biaggi started well again but after just a few corners was passed by Haga who set a new track record on lap 3. Ben Spies was third in the early stages but then took Biaggi and set off after the Japanese rider. Corser raised a few eyebrows with an early fourth place, but then Kiyonari

# WSBK Championship

*Nori Haga (41) managed to limit the damage by twice finishing runner-up on the Ducati. The real revelation however was the Aprilia, which scored its first podium in just its third race, thanks to Max Biaggi.*

took over in that position for Ten Kate. Spies flashed past Haga on the line at the end of lap 5 to take the lead, and took over as the new track record holder. Behind the American Biaggi also passed the Ducati while Kiyonari was getting closer. A third of the way into the race, Spies already had a one-second lead over the rest, which became two when they reached the mid-point. Haga, Biaggi and Kiyonari were all bunched together, while even Sykes was unsuccessfully trying to latch onto them. The race continued without any more surprises until the end except for the scrap for second place between Biaggi and Haga, with the Japanese rider repeating his race 1 result. The podium was the same, while Kiyonari scored an encouraging fourth place. In the world championship Haga was leading with 85 points, ten more than Spies; Neukirchner was already some way behind on 40, with Biaggi on 38, Haslam on 36, Sykes on 32, and Laconi and Rea on 30.

WSBK Races

Arai
SHARK
VOLVO
YAMAHA
PARTS EUROPE
66
alpinestars
xerox
41
DUCATI
BREIL MILANO
V-Power
valsir
xerox
V-Power
BREIL MILANO

# (05.04) Valencia (ESP)

Ben Spies slammed in another of his trademark quick laps at Valencia to set the new circuit record. Despite a technical glitch that brought his progress to a halt during Superpole 2, he returned to the pits, went out again five minutes before the end of the session and clinched the pole.

Alongside Spies could be found three Ducatis, the best one of which was Regis Laconi with the DFX 1098R. The Frenchman administered his tyres well and went out at the very end to set a quick time.

It was the opposite however for the factory bikes which only went out in the second half of the final run, taking front row positions with Haga and Fabrizio.

## RACE 1

Haga 'wheelied' across the finish line as the winner and with a comfortable advantage over his rivals who were almost four seconds behind.

After a scrap with Neukirchner in the early laps, the Ducati man gradually pulled away to take an easy win.

Ducati's superb race was completed with a second place for Michel Fabrizio, who recovered well after a poor start and eventually took Neukirchner for the runner-up slot on lap 21.

The German finished third and was now third in the championship standings. It was an unfortunate race for Spies who was running in third when he crashed at the first curve on lap 10 after getting on the throttle too quickly.

The Yamaha man was visibly disappointed but kept hold of second place in the table.

Laconi had a fantastic race with the private Ducati, the Frenchman staying with the leaders throughout and then fighting with Kagayama for fourth.

Leon Haslam also went well on the Honda, attacking throughout to finish in fifth place. Biaggi started a bit behind and did what he could on a track where overtaking is not easy. In the end he finished in eighth place, taking his score to 46, one less than Haslam.

Haga meanwhile had increased his lead in the table and was now on 110 points.

## RACE 2

The second Valencia race was rather monotonous as Haga dominated to the flag.

# WSBK Championship

### Race 1

| | | | |
|---|---|---|---|
| 1° | N. Haga | (JPN - Ducati) | 36'44"766 |
| | | | 150,408 km/h |
| 2° | M. Fabrizio | (ITA - Ducati) | + 3"677 |
| 3° | M. Neukirchner | (GER - Suzuki) | +3"959 |
| 4° | R. Laconi | (FRA - Ducati) | + 4"210 |
| 5° | L. Haslam | (GBR - Honda) | + 13"824 |

### Race 2

| | | | |
|---|---|---|---|
| 1° | N. Haga | (JPN - Ducati) | 36'46"927 |
| | | | 150,261 km/h |
| 2° | B. Spies | (USA - Yamaha) | + 5"105 |
| 3° | M. Fabrizio | (ITA - Ducati) | + 6"386 |
| 4° | R. Laconi | (FRA - Ducati) | + 6"573 |
| 5° | L. Haslam | (GBR - Honda) | + 14"075 |

After letting Neukirchner get a look-in during the early laps, the Japanese rider moved into the lead, leaving his rivals over five seconds behind. Nitro-Nori had now proved to be getting the hang of his Ducati 1098R.

After his DNF in race 1 Ben Spies started to think about the points as he was 40 adrift of Haga, and he settled for second ahead of the other Ducati Xerox rider.

Fabrizio scored another podium and was rapidly moving up to the top part of the table, in fourth place with 60 points.

Regis Laconi was once again a protagonist in race 2: with a private Ducati he was up with the leaders but a few hairy moments convinced him to settle for another fourth place.

Leon Haslam was the top CBR 1000 RR runner, again winning the in-house duel with his team-mate John Hopkins.

The American managed to get inside the top 10 but in the end finished in twelfth place.

Out of the other Honda runners Carlos Checa finished in sixth, a full 17 seconds behind the winner, and his Ten Kate team-mate Kiyonari was ninth.

Neukirchner dropped off considerably, slipping down to seventh place at the flag but he was still third in the points table, just in front of Fabrizio. Biaggi came home in eighth place after passing a few of his rivals in the early laps and then getting embroiled in a battle with Hopkins, Sykes and Kiyonari.

The Aprilia man got the better of all three of them and was now seventh with 54 points.

≡ *Ducati, with both its riders on the podium (Michel Fabrizio, 84 and Noriyuki Haga, 41), responded to Yamaha, who only scored a second place with Spies. Neukirchner (75) and Laconi (55) also went well.*

# (24.04)
# Assen (NL)

**B**en Spies continued his exceptional run of qualifying form by destroying the lap record at Assen, another track that before Friday had been completely unknown to him. The Texan smashed Bayliss's old record by seven-tenths of a second, and even Jakub Smrz with the private Guandalini Ducati went under the old mark, as well as Haslam and the two factory Ducati riders.

## RACE 1

Spies got the best start and soon pulled away together with Max Neukirchner, while Haga chased after them. Michel Fabrizio (Ducati Xerox) and Max Biaggi (Aprilia) were the other protagonists of the early laps, while the others were some way behind. On lap 5 Checa crashed out, while Haslam moved closer to the front.

Lap 7 saw Neukirchner crash out as well, the German got back in the race but was out of contention and then two laps later Haga concluded his chase by latching onto Spies's tail. At the mid-point Spies and Haga were together, followed by Haslam, while Sykes was almost six seconds behind and Biaggi nine. On lap 13 Haga passed Spies and moved into the lead; shortly after Haslam also overtook the American who was saving his tyres for the run-in.

On lap 14 Nakano crashed out of the points as well, while Fabrizio lost a couple of places. With a third of the race still to run, Haga had a 3/10 of a second lead over Haslam and 5/10 over Spies. In the last few nail-biting laps, Spies was back with Haslam and two from the end put on a terrific elbow-to-elbow scrap with his British rival. At this point the American moved ahead and set off after Haga who was still in the lead.

On the last lap Spies tried to pass at all costs but Haga's precision was perfect in every curve. Three laps from the end the American passed him with a superb copybook move to take his fourth win of the year. Haslam had a superb race together with these two champions, but had to settle for third with fastest lap.

The others were some way behind, headed by Sykes who in turn had shaken off a determined Biaggi. After a good start Fabrizio lost out in the battle for eighth to Troy Corser on the BMW.

### Race 1

| | | | |
|---|---|---|---|
| 1° | B. Spies | (USA - Yamaha) | 36'31"338 |
| | | | 164,628 km/h |
| 2° | N. Haga | (JPN - Ducati) | + 0"154 |
| 3° | L. Haslam | (GBR - Honda) | + 0"779 |
| 4° | T. Sykes | (GBR - Yamaha) | + 8"775 |
| 5° | M. Biaggi | (ITA - Aprilia) | + 11"275 |

### Race 2

| | | | |
|---|---|---|---|
| 1° | N. Haga | (JPN - Ducati) | 36'31"712 |
| | | | 164,6 km/h |
| 2° | L. Haslam | (GBR - Honda) | + 2"678 |
| 3° | J. Smrz | (CZE - Ducati) | + 4"603 |
| 4° | M. Fabrizio | (ITA - Ducati) | + 8"981 |
| 5° | J. Rea | (GBR - Honda) | + 12"104 |

*After winning race 1 Ben Spies made an incredible error in race 2, leaving the door open for Haga who pulled ahead in the points.*

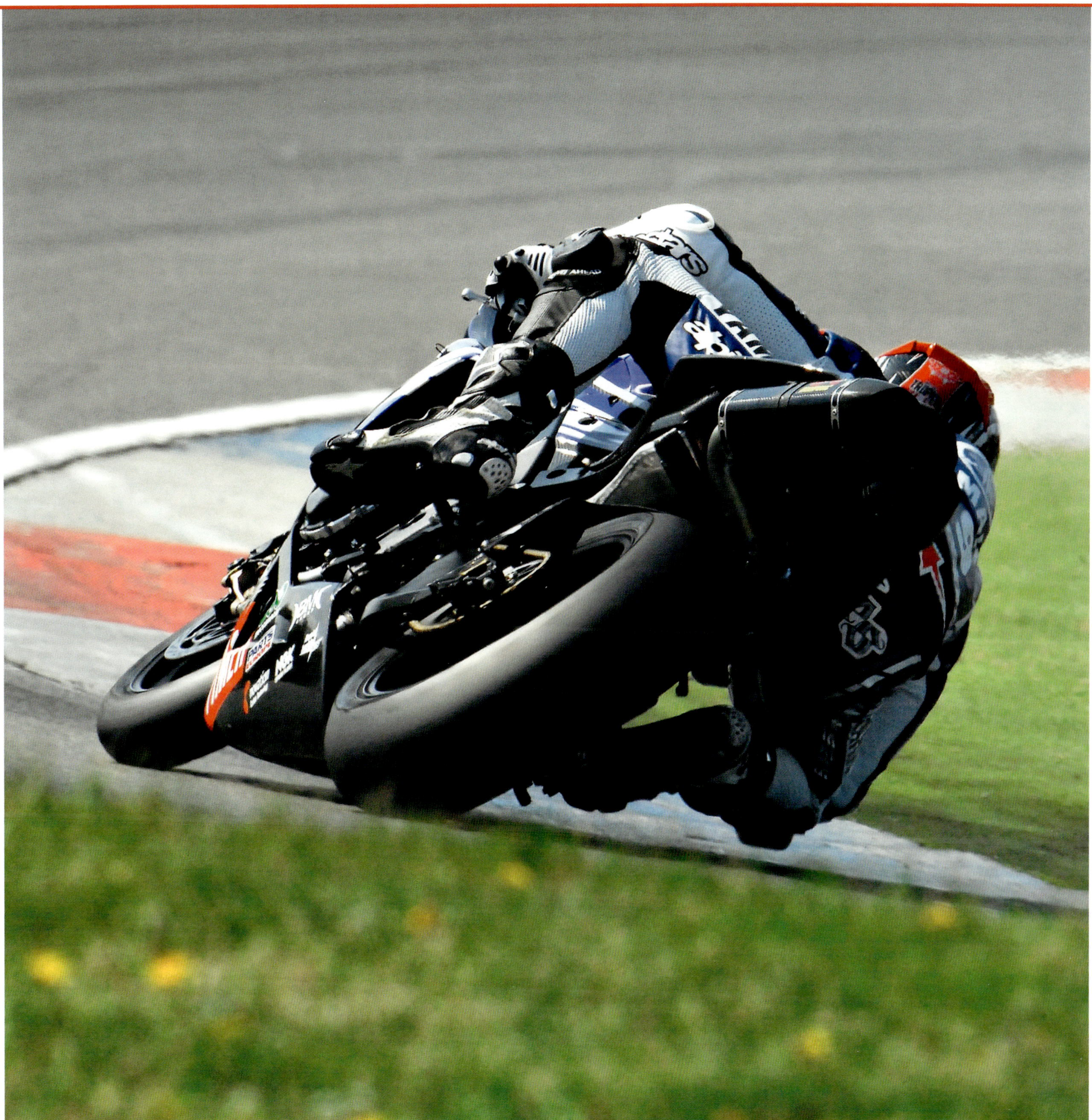

96
JENSEN MOTORSPORTS
EMILIANA SERBATOI

MARTINI
ADVANCE
GNUTTI

# WSBK Championship

## RACE 2

At the end of lap 1 Biaggi returned to the pits with a broken clutch, depriving the race of one of its protagonists but the real upset came on lap 2 when Spies flew off the track at turn 3 and destroyed his Yamaha. Haga continued in the lead followed at a short distance by Neukirchner and Haslam, while Fabrizio also latched onto these three and then the German overshot and lost three positions. Haga increased his lead to over two seconds and Fabrizio, who was now in second, was controlling Haslam, Smrz and Neukirchner. Haga continued his solitary ride up at the front and increased his lead as the race went on. Half-way through Haslam passed Fabrizio who now had to deal with Smrz, while Rea and Sykes were having a terrific scrap for fifth place. In the final stages Haslam pulled out a gap on his adversaries, Fabrizio and Smrz, despite a gap of over four seconds from the leader Haga. The two Ducati riders were gearing up for a sprint finish, which played out in favour of Smrz, thanks also to a broken gearbox on the Italian's bike.

The world championship now saw Haga in the lead with 180 points against 120 for Spies and 94 for Haslam, who overtook Michel Fabrizio on 80. Biaggi was seventh with 75 points.

*With a first and a second place Haga (previous page, celebrating with champagne) managed to increase his lead over Spies. The unlucky Neukirchner (75) crashed out, while Leon Haslam (91) scored two podiums. Jakub Smrz (96) also went well with a private Ducati, scoring a third place in race 2.*

# (10.05) Monza (ITA)

With a fantastic lap in the final Superpole run, Spies notched up a time of 1 minute 44.073 seconds that enabled him to take his fifth successive pole position. The American didn't use his Q-tyre in the first run and then bolted on his second in the final stages of the last run, ready to see off any eventual attacks from Ducati, seeing as Michel Fabrizio had been the quickest throughout the sessions. The Italian however was only a couple of tenths off the pace of Spies, and would start from the front row together with Kiyonari, who took Honda back to the front again, and Neukirchner with the Suzuki; four different makes on the first row, and a guaranteed spectacle.

Haga was unable to get under the 1'45'' mark despite setting a good pace on race tyres, and he had to settle for the second row alongside Jonathan Rea (Hannspree Ten Kate Honda), Max Biaggi (Aprilia Racing), who set a record Superbike top speed at 325.8 km/h, and Kagayama.

## RACE 1

Shortly after the start a multiple crash at the first chicane saw several riders go down in a nasty fashion. In the first Roberts and Tamada touched on the outside of the group. The Japanese rider crashed on the grass, while the Australian continued his race and involuntarily brought down Max Neukirchner.

At the same time in the middle of the field, Tommy Hill made contact with another rider, causing a multiple crash that also involved Corser and Checa. Several riders were on the ground but they were seen to immediately, while the red flags came out after a couple of minutes to stop the race.

On the restart Fabrizio was quick off the mark and took the lead from Haga, who had entered the first chicane first. On lap 5 the Rome man and his Japanese team-mate were caught by Spies, who moved into the lead on the following lap. At the two-thirds point Fabrizio was again right behind Spies together with Haga, and the two Ducati riders, while constantly swapping places, did not obstruct each other and took over at the front until lap 17, when Spies made his move.

WSBK Races

WSBK Races

# WSBK Championship

The last few laps were a tremendous battle between the three, but Spies's Yamaha ran out of fuel half-way through the final Parabolica curve on the final lap, leaving the win to Fabrizio ahead of Haga.

There could have been two Italians on the podium but Max Biaggi, who finished third, was penalized by 20 seconds by the Race Direction for cutting the chicane and was relegated to eleventh place. It was a real shame because Biaggi ran an excellent race once again.

Third place therefore went to Kiyonari with the Ten Kate Honda, ahead of Kagayama (Suzuki) and Rea (Honda), while Xaus had a good run to finish seventh for BMW.

## RACE 2

Spies made amends by dominating race 2 at Monza following his first race disappointment.

The American took the flag by a comfortable margin, but slowed down towards the end, maybe to save fuel, and won the race by 2.5 seconds

After his race 1 win Fabrizio settled for the runner-up slot, but he had to work hard to defend it from Kiyonari.

Johnny Rea scored another good result for the Ten Kate team with fourth place, finishing ahead of Biaggi in fifth, while Haslam finished seventh

Ruben Xaus also put together a good race with his BMW, fighting for eighth place with Checa, Smrz and Laconi.

However the big news was that the points leader Noriyuki Haga crashed out on lap 4, giving a big advantage to Spies. Thanks to his win in race 2, the Texan was now only 54 points behind his Ducati rival. Fabrizio was third, 75 points behind his team-mate.

*First win in his career for Fabrizio, after Spies (19) had run out of fuel at the last corner. The American made amends in race 2. As well as the spectacular crash at the first chicane, Monza also saw good performances from Haga (41), Biaggi (3) and Kiyonari (9).*

### Race 1

| | | | |
|---|---|---|---|
| 1° | M. Fabrizio | (ITA - Ducati) | 31'50"758 |
| | | | 196,459 km/h |
| 2° | N. Haga | (JPN - Ducati) | + 0"239 |
| 3° | R. Kiyonari | (JPN - Honda) | + 8"175 |
| 4° | Y. Kagayama | (JPN - Suzuki) | + 11"001 |
| 5° | J. Rea | (GBR - Honda) | + 12"447 |

### Race 2

| | | | |
|---|---|---|---|
| 1° | B. Spies | (USA - Yamaha) | 31'49"252 |
| | | | 196,614 km/h |
| 2° | M. Fabrizio | (ITA - Ducati) | + 2"665 |
| 3° | R. Kiyonari | (JPN - Honda) | + 2"810 |
| 4° | J. Rea | (GBR - Honda) | + 7"706 |
| 5° | M. Biaggi | (ITA - Aprilia) | + 7"863 |

PIRELLI
alpinestars
PIRELLI
DUCATI CORSE
xerox
Superbike Team
ADVANCE
valsir
ADVANCE
xerox
MILANO
valsir
SUPERBIKE

# Kyalami (ZA) (17•05)

### Race 1

| | | | |
|---|---|---|---|
| 1° | N. Haga | (JPN - Ducati) | 39'47"436 |
| | | | 153,66 km/h |
| 2° | M. Fabrizio | (ITA - Ducati) | + 0"950 |
| 3° | B. Spies | (USA - Yamaha) | + 3"391 |
| 4° | J. Rea | (GBR - Honda) | + 8"914 |
| 5° | M. Biaggi | (ITA - Aprilia) | + 9"019 |

### Race 2

| | | | |
|---|---|---|---|
| 1° | N. Haga | (JPN - Ducati) | 39'45"027 |
| | | | 153,816 km/h |
| 2° | M. Fabrizio | (ITA - Ducati) | + 0"322 |
| 3° | J. Rea | (GBR - Honda) | + 8"936 |
| 4° | L. Haslam | (GBR - Honda) | + 10"561 |
| 5° | M. Biaggi | (ITA - Aprilia) | + 10"767 |

*Nori Haga scored an amazing double win in South Africa. Ducati's Japanese rider now had an 88 point lead in the points table.*

Just one thousandth of a second in Superpole split Ben Spies and Michel Fabrizio, who waged war in the last few moments in an effort to take the top slot on the grid. Yamaha's American rookie scored his sixth successive pole, equalling this particular Superbike record held by Doug Polen (Ducati). The front row was completed by Max Biaggi and Noriyuki Haga, who grabbed the fourth place despite still suffering from a painful arm he picked up when he was hit by a pigeon at Monza.

Regis Laconi crashed during the opening lap of free practice between turns 11 and 12 and suffered a severe trauma to the vertebrae. The French rider's condition was serious and the medics immediately air-lifted him to hospital. The DFX team rider was operated on and returned to France to begin a lengthy rehabilitation period.

### RACE 1

Haga got the best start, followed by Biaggi who was passed by Spies on the inside of Turn 1, while Fabrizio was fourth. At the end of lap 1 the positions were Haga, Fabrizio, Spies, Checa, Rea and Biaggi, and then on lap 2 Fabrizio took over the lead of the race from Haga.

With a third gone Fabrizio continued to set a record pace, while behind there was a scrap between Checa and Biaggi for fifth place, which appeared to be going in favour of the Italian.

At the mid-point the positions were unchanged even though Haga was upping the ante and in fact he then took over at the front from Fabrizio. Spies was over a second behind, then came Rea with a gap of four seconds and Biaggi with six.

At two-thirds distance there was now a trio in the lead with Haga followed by Fabrizio and Spies: the American then passed the Italian on lap 17 and set about catching the leader, taking Michel with him. The battle between these two played to Haga's advantage and the Japanese rider managed to gain over a second on his pursuers.

On lap 20 Spies got things a bit wrong and Fabrizio took back second place, while behind Biaggi had caught Rea and was aiming at fourth place.

With Haga unable to be caught, Fabrizio firmly in second place and Spies settling for third, the race came to a close without any further excitement. Biaggi tried to pass Rea right until the final curve but had to settle for fifth place.

*With two second places Michel Fabrizio (84) overtook Ben Spies (19) in the standings.*

*The American, who was on the podium in race 1, had a DNF in the second race.*

*Jonathan Rea (65) had an excellent race on his Ten Kate Honda, battling with Max Biaggi (3).*

## RACE 2

Once again Haga rocketed off the line to take the lead but this time Spies was not caught unawares and he slotted in behind Nitro-Nori on lap 2. But the real upset came during the third lap when Spies suddenly sat up on the bike, his engine KO, then pulled into the pits and retired.

Haga at this point had a one-second lead on Rea who was passed on lap 4 by Fabrizio. Biaggi was in fourth position and was aiming to pass the Honda rider, while Leon Haslam was behind them.

Half-way through the race Fabrizio was right behind Haga and a duel was on the cards while behind Haslam passed Biaggi who went a bit wide in the turn before the finish line and let the British rider through.

The last few laps were relatively quiet as Fabrizio decided to settle for the championship points and not hassle team-mate Haga who could consolidate his lead. Behind there was a great tussle between Rea and Haslam, while Biaggi was playing a tactical game and waiting for the right moment to strike. Rea didn't want any surprises from a rider of the calibre of Max, and he stepped on the gas, leaving the Italian to battle with Haslam.

On the last lap there were two surprises: the first was when Haga hesitated while he was lapping the wild-card, Whyte, and Fabrizio tried to pass him but couldn't make it. The second was at the corner before the finish-line, when Haga came in a bit too hard and this time Fabrizio passed him, but he went wide and Haga retook him again. The win, his second of the day, went to Noriyuki, but Fabrizio was a worthy second. Rea was third while Biaggi was unable to pass Haslam and had to settle for fifth place ahead of Checa and Nakano.

In the points table Haga now had 250, and was some way ahead of Fabrizio on 165 and Spies on 162. Haslam was next up with 116, Rea with 106 and Biaggi and Sykes on 103.

sterilgarda
YAMAHA
FIMER
19
alpinestars

HANNspree
65
ids
Arai
3
RIFLE

WSBK Races

# (31.05) Miller (USA)

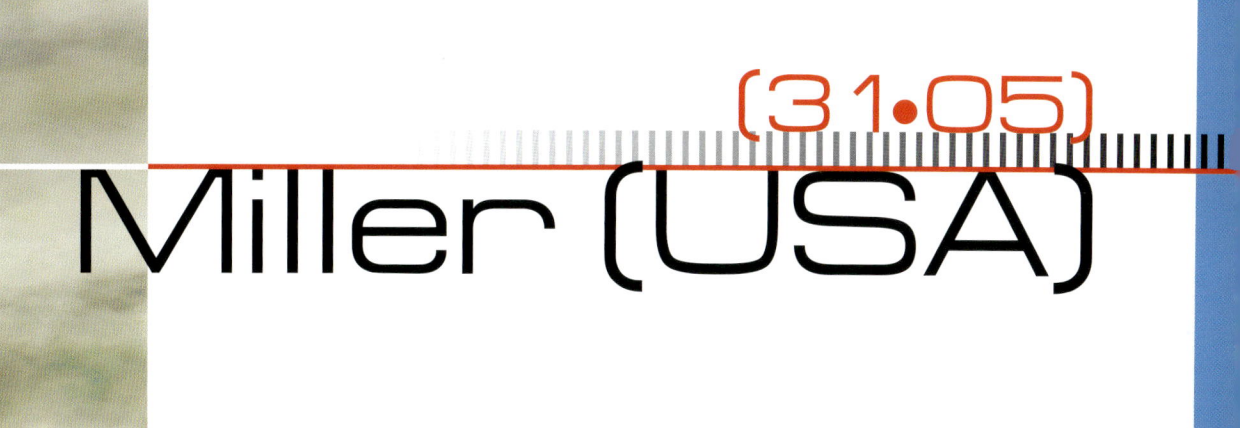

Ben Spies took his seventh pole position in a row for Yamaha, seeing off Carlos Checa (Honda) by almost six-tenths and Kiyonari by almost a second. Fabrizio had to settle for the final front row grid slot, while Haga was only ninth and Biaggi crashed in Superpole 2 after touching the kerbing with his footpeg. He was taken back to the pits, where he grabbed his second bike with three minutes to go, but he could only complete one lap and qualified in sixteenth place.

## RACE 1

Spies rocketed off the line and soon put some considerable space between himself and the rest of the field: at the first split he was more than a second ahead and two seconds by the end of lap 1!! Behind Nakano (Aprilia) was in terrific form and headed two other Japanese riders Kiyonari and Haga; Parkes with the Kawasaki was fifth ahead of Checa, Fabrizio and Biaggi. Spies increased his lead by around one second a lap until Kiyonari got past Nakano and set off after the American. Further behind Fabrizio was getting into the swing of things and soon latched onto the chasing trio of Kiyonari, Checa and Nakano.

On lap 7 Muggeridge crashed and the Race Direction brought out the red flags to allow medical assistance for the Australian rider, who only had a few bruises.

The standings in this first part of the race, taken at the end of lap 5 as per the regulations, saw Spies in the lead followed by Kiyonari, Nakano, Checa, Fabrizio and Haga; Biaggi was ninth. On the restart Spies again powered away to lead but this time he was shadowed by Kiyonari who passed him a few corners later! But the Texan was soon back in front and with a fantastic second lap pulled out over Checa, who in the meantime had passed Kiyo-san. Biaggi was in sixth place, with the two Ducatis behind.

The race continued with Spies comfortably in the lead and with a second and a half over Checa, but the lead was actually six seconds on aggregate. It was no contest....

Fron lap 5 onwards Fabrizio began a superb recovery that saw him pass Haga, then Haslam and finally the Kawasaki pair of Hacking and Parkes.

While Spies continued to be the 'Lone Rider' up front, followed by Checa and Rea,

# WSBK Championship

*Ben Spies was untouchable at his home round and not even Michel Fabrizio (84, in a fight with Biaggi) managed to get close to the American. Carlos Checa (7), double winner in 2008, had to settle for second place in race 1, while Johnny Rea (65) also went well.*

### Race 1

| | | | |
|---|---|---|---|
| 1° | B. Spies | (USA - Yamaha) | 38'30"945 |
| | | | 160,527 km/h |
| 2° | C. Checa | (ESP - Honda) | + 9"394 |
| 3° | M. Fabrizio | (ITA - Ducati) | + 12"742 |
| 4° | R. Kiyonari | (JPN - Honda) | + 14"276 |
| 5° | J. Rea | (GBR - Honda) | + 14"915 |

### Race 2

| | | | |
|---|---|---|---|
| 1° | B. Spies | (USA - Yamaha) | 38'25"391 |
| | | | 160,914 km/h |
| 2° | M. Fabrizio | (ITA - Ducati) | + 9"080 |
| 3° | J. Rea | (GBR - Honda) | + 14"357 |
| 4° | M. Biaggi | (ITA - Aprilia) | + 15"636 |
| 5° | R. Kiyonari | (JPN - Honda) | + 17"156 |

Biaggi caught and passed Kiyonari to move into fourth. Fabrizio was in sixth and then passed the Japanese rider on lap 18. Two laps later the Ducati man caught and passed Biaggi to take the final podium place on aggregate. Spies took the flag by more than four seconds in the second part and nine overall. Behind the American finished Checa, Rea and Fabrizio, but on aggregate this changed to Checa, Fabrizio, Kiyonari, Rea and Biaggi.

## RACE 2

Spies again got a good start but so did Fabrizio and Checa, as well as Biaggi and Haga. But the mere thought that anyone could trouble the American didn't last long, less than one lap in fact: at the end of lap 1 Spies already had eight-tenths of a second lead over Fabrizio who was about to be caught by Checa, but the Spanish rider crashed out of the race immediately after.

The real spectacle was on offer however by the group battling for third place: Rea, Biaggi, Kiyonari, Haslam, Haga and Smrz were all in single file waiting for the last few laps to make their move.

Two-thirds of the way through the Hondas were the first to go as Rea, Haslam and Kiyonari decided to fight it out in the family for the final podium place.

Biaggi also moved into the battle with three laps left, while up at the front Fabrizio attempate to catch Spies but then rolled off the throttle to settle for the 20 points.

On the last lap Haslam crashed and it was Rea who took the final podium place.

In the table Haga was at the top with 265 points, but his lead was now reduced: Spies was on 212 and Fabrizio 201. Rea was now ahead of Haslam in fourth, while Biaggi was still in sixth place.

WSBK Races

# (21.06)
# Misano (RSM)

Ben Spies's Superpole domination came to an end at Misano with a surprising exploit by Jakub Smrz. The young rider from the Czech Republic powered his private Guandalini Ducati machine to the top slot, ahead of all the factory teams and setting the new circuit record in the process.

Alongside on the front row were Britain's Jonathan Rea, who was galvanized by the latest improvements to his Honda, and two of the men chasing the title, Ben Spies and Michel Fabrizio. Noriyuki Haga on the other hand would start from row 2.

### RACE 1

At the start it was Byrne with the Sterilgarda Ducati who shot into the lead, the British rider immediately pulling away from Smrz on the other private 1098. Behind could be found Fabrizio, who was followed by Spies. All the riders started on rain tyres, which shook matters up somewhat, and Ruben Xaus was looking comfortable in seventh place on the BMW.

On lap 10, the flag-to-flag rule meant that riders could come in and change bikes and the first to do so was Nakano, followed by Haga. Carlos Checa and Ruben Xaus however continued to lap at a good pace on rain tyres and they would be the last riders to come in and change.

Just after half-distance, almost all the top men had changed their bikes and the times were now coming down rapidly, but ahead Byrne, Checa, Smrz and Xaus in particular were lapping quickly even on rain tyres. On lap 16 Checa and Smrz came in for their change, but the Spaniard had a few problems in restarting (as had happened to Rea) and came back into the race in sixteenth place.

On the next lap Byrne came in, leaving the BMW of Xaus in the lead, but after changing his bike Ben Spies was now on a lap record pace and easily passed Xaus to take the lead.

At this point Spies was just 38 points behind Haga in the table but the Japanese rider tried to pass those ahead of him in an attempt to limit the damage. For his part Fabrizio was in third, while Xaus had been caught speeding in the pitlane as he came in to change and was given a ride-through penalty.

In the final stages Smrz came very close to Fabrizio, but the Italian succeeded in holding onto the final podium place. Haga meanwhile managed to grab fifth on the final lap, which helped him gain another point on Spies.

### Race 1

| | | | |
|---|---|---|---|
| 1° | B. Spies | (USA - Yamaha) | 45'02"773 |
| | | | 135,093 km/h |
| 2° | S. Byrne | (GBR - Ducati) | + 7"931 |
| 3° | M. Fabrizio | (ITA - Ducati) | + 11"836 |
| 4° | J. Smrz | (CZE - Ducati) | + 11"886 |
| 5° | N. Haga | (JPN - Ducati) | + 31"670 |

### Race 2

| | | | |
|---|---|---|---|
| 1° | J. Rea | (GBR - Honda) | 39'11"204 |
| | | | 155,293 km/h |
| 2° | M. Fabrizio | (ITA - Ducati) | + 0"63 |
| 3° | N. Haga | (JPN - Ducati) | + 0"457 |
| 4° | J. Smrz | (CZE - Ducati) | + 3"635 |
| 5° | C. Checa | (ESP - Honda) | + 4"460 |

*A superb Jonathan Rea scored the first win of his WSB career at Misano on the Ten Kate Honda CBR 1000 RR. The British rider fought off and defeated a swathe of Ducati riders who finished behind him.*

Red Bull
HANNspree
65
ids
Hanns·G
HONDA
PIRELLI
ARROW
Castrol

96
Arai
PIRELLI
BOULDER

SHOEI
67
19
sterilgarda
PATA

xerox
valsir
BREIL
ADVANCE
DUCATI
1198
PIRELLI

# WSBK Championship

## RACE 2

This time the factory Ducatis got the best start, while Jonathan Rea managed to get his Honda in between the two and Smrz latched on to the leading trio. Spies was fifth but on lap 4 raised his hand immediately after the finish line, looking down at the left rear of his Yamaha machine. The American slipped down to sixteenth place but a couple of laps later began to lap at a good pace once more.

In the meantime Rea had moved into the lead, followed by the three Ducatis. Haga and Fabrizio were scrapping for second place but they were holding each other up allowing the Honda man to get away. In the meantime Smrz got it all wrong and lost three places. Half-way through the race Haga passed Fabrizio and the Japanese rider latched onto the rear of Rea. A few laps later Fabrizio also cut loose and moved into the lead with a fantastic pass on his British opponent.

The final laps were nail-biting, with Fabrizio and Rea constantly trying to outbrake each other into the corners, while Haga continued in third, waiting for any false move by the leading duo and thinking of the points.

On the final lap Jonathan Rea powered his way past Fabrizio immediately after the finish line. In the next three corners the Ducati man tried to get back in the lead again, but the 22 year-old from Ballymena had things under control and took the chequered flag for his first win in Superbike and confirming the progress made by the Hondas.

With third place Noriyuki Haga consolidated his points lead (292 points), Fabrizio was now on 237, while Spies made an exceptional recovery to gain seven points for ninth and was now on 244.

*Ducati had to take second best to Honda and Yamaha, settling for the podium slots with factory riders Fabrizio and Haga and privateer Byrne (67). Smrz (96) scored two excellent fourth places. Race 1 saw another win for Spies (19) but the weather conditions made things uncertain right throughout.*

# (28.06) Donington (GBR)

A few drops of rain in the final stages managed to ruin a fantastic Superpole which was proving to be full of surprises. With a time set just a few instants before it began to rain, Ben Spies succeeded in grabbing the best lap (but not the record) and took his tally to eight out of nine Superpoles this year. The American was ahead of Max Biaggi who confirmed his love of this circuit and Shane Byrne with the Sterilgarda Ducati machine. The second Aprilia of Nakano completed the front row. The two factory Ducatis started from row 2 together with the Honda of Carlos Checa and the Ducati of Jakub Smrz.

## RACE 1

Spies got the best start to lead, followed by Biaggi and Haga, while Fabrizio got an awful start that dropped him to tenth place. The leading trio pulled away, then on lap 5, Nitro-Nori lost ground and the battle was now between Spies and Biaggi. The Yamaha man tried on numerous occasions to shake off his Italian rival.

Behind them Byrne was caught by Haslam and Nakano, while Fabrizio first managed to get up to seventh place but was then passed by Rea.

Half-way through Spies had half a second lead over Biaggi, while Haga was almost four seconds off the pace. The trio of Byrne, Haslam and Nakano were next up over 11 seconds behind. For his part Fabrizio continued to lose ground and was even passed by Hopkins and Smrz.

Max Biaggi at the second split was getting closer and closer to Spies, one tenth was the minimum margin, and matters between the two looked to be coming to a head. On the last lap Spies put things beyond reach by slamming in a sub-1m31s time and went on to win, while Biaggi had a technical glitch which then disappeared almost immediately and the Italian was able to finish runner-up ahead of Haga almost 11 seconds behind. Haslam and Byrne had a sprint finish to the line, finishing in that order ahead of Nakano.

## RACE 2

Biaggi was quickest off the mark but already at the first curve Ben Spies powered past him into the lead. Haga tried to keep up and latched onto Nakano who had moved into third.

WSBK Races

enigma
HONDA
91
Arai

xerox
84
DUCATI
BREIL
valsir
ADVANCE
1198

xerox
1198
valsir
ADVANCE
BREIL
MILANO
PIRELLI
DUCATI

# WSBK Championship

Aprilia's Japanese rider then crashed on lap 2, immediately imitated by Rea who managed to remount and get back into the race.
On lap 5 Biaggi ended up on the track at the Melbourne hairpin, and when he got going again he made contact with Camier but without any consequences. Half a lap further up the track and it was Haga who crashed out, followed on the next lap by Carlos Checa.
Ducati's Japanese rider crashed violently however and as he went off onto the gravel he was hit by his bike. Taken to the Medical Centre he was diagnosed as having a fractured vertebra, and then in hospital underwent a CT scan that showed the injury was not so serious. However he also suffered a broken bone in his right arm in the crash, and after fears that he would be out for the next two or three races, Nori began R & R for his return at Brno.

A third of the way through Spies had over five seconds lead on Fabrizio, who was, by a stroke of luck, right behind the Texan. The Ducati rider however had to watch out for Leon Haslam who was not giving up one instant.
Spies' seven-second lead at the mid-point was almost embarrassing for his rivals. Haslam, Byrne and Fabrizio were fighting for the other podium positions, followed at a distance by Sykes.
The race did not provide any other excitement, and the positions remained the same, with the exception of Fabrizio who moved back into third place behind Haslam for another podium.
In the championship Haga was still at the top on 308 points, but now just 14 ahead of Spies who had almost concluded his incredible recovery. Fabrizio was third on 257.

*Another double win for Spies (19) who shared the race 1 podium with Biaggi (3) and Haga (41). The Japanese rider crashed in race 2, while Fabrizio (84) stepped onto the podium. Haslam (91) was on form and took a top 5 finish in both races.*

### Race 1
|    |           |                |            |
|----|-----------|----------------|------------|
| 1° | B. Spies  | (USA - Yamaha) | 34'57"230  |
|    |           |                | 158,831 km/h |
| 2° | M. Biaggi | (ITA - Aprilia)| + 7"156    |
| 3° | N. Haga   | (JPN - Ducati) | + 10"968   |
| 4° | L. Haslam | (GBR - Honda)  | + 18"843   |
| 5° | S. Byrne  | (GBR - Ducati) | + 19"125   |

### Race 2
|    |            |                |            |
|----|------------|----------------|------------|
| 1° | B. Spies   | (USA - Yamaha) | 35'14"788  |
|    |            |                | 157,512 km/h |
| 2° | L. Haslam  | (GBR - Honda)  | + 6"622    |
| 3° | M. Fabrizio| (ITA - Ducati) | + 6"816    |
| 4° | S. Byrne   | (GBR - Ducati) | + 7"349    |
| 5° | T. Sykes   | (GBR - Yamaha) | + 8"145    |

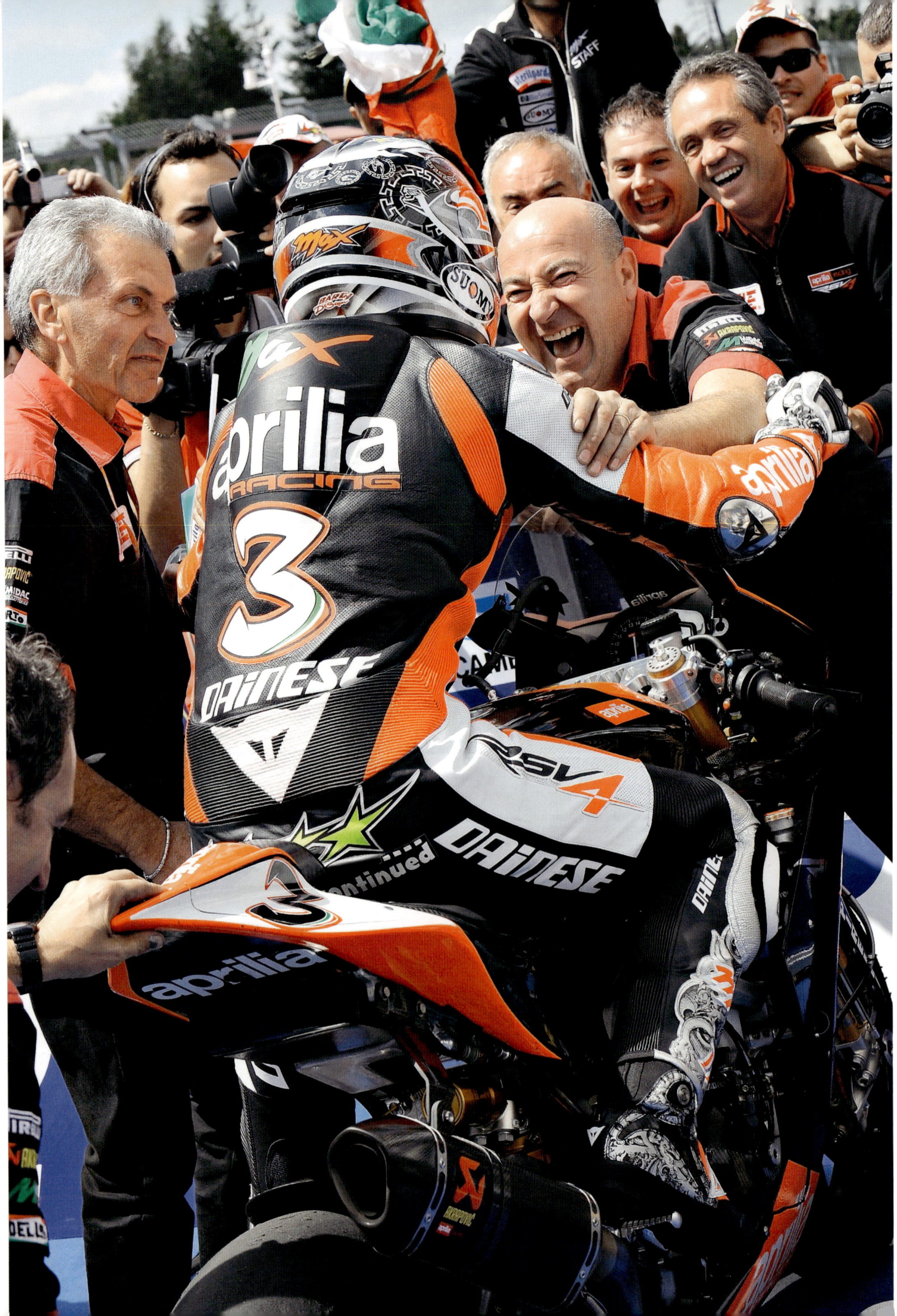
aprilia
RACING
3
DAINESE
SUOMY
RSV4
DAINESE
aprilia

# Brno (Czech Rep.) (26.07)

| Race 1 | | | |
|---|---|---|---|
| 1° | M. Biaggi | (ITA – Aprilia) | 40'18"306 |
| | | | 160,863 km/h |
| 2° | C. Checa | (ESP – Honda) | + 3"631 |
| 3° | J. Rea | (GBR – Honda) | + 9"948 |
| 4° | S. Byrne | (GBR – Ducati) | + 12"952 |
| 5° | T. Corser | (AUS – BMW) | + 14"599 |

| Race 2 | | | |
|---|---|---|---|
| 1° | B. Spies | (USA – Yamaha) | 40'15"420 |
| | | | 161,055 km/h |
| 2° | M. Biaggi | (ITA – Aprilia) | + 0"213 |
| 3° | M. Fabrizio | (ITA – Ducati) | + 0"657 |
| 4° | J. Rea | (GBR – Honda) | + 8"311 |
| 5° | C. Checa | (ESP – Honda) | + 8"915 |

*Max Biaggi and Aprilia scored a superb win at the Czech Republic circuit. The Italian bike is in its first season of WSB racing.*

Ben Spies powered to his ninth Superpole pole position of the year ahead of Michel Fabrizio and Max Biaggi who had to settle for second and third on the starting-grid. Jonathan Rea completed the front row with the Ten Kate Honda, while the two BMWs of Corser and Xaus were alongside Byrne on row 2 together with Sykes.

## RACE 1

To see a BMW in the lead of a WSB race was a truly exciting moment. It happened in the early laps, when Troy Corser got ahead of Ben Spies, Max Biaggi and Michel Fabrizio. The American took over at the front, the Italian was right on his exhausts and so was Fabrizio in third. Corser was still there however in fourth place, shadowed by the two Hondas of Rea and Checa. Xaus crashed out of the front positions and damaged his hip.

On lap 4 a reckless move by Fabrizio on Spies eliminated both riders from the race. Biaggi inherited the lead and the Italian was able to hold off Checa, Rea and Corser. This double elimination helped to favour Haga in eighth place, the Japanese rider battling with Haslam, Tamada and Smrz.

Biaggi, who was keeping up easily with Spies and Fabrizio before they bowed out of the race, continued his solitary ride up front, controlling Checa who in turn was being hassled by Rea. A little distance behind Corser was scrapping with Byrne, who passed him with a third of the race still to go.

No one was able to trouble Max Biaggi, who managed to administer his two second lead and take the Aprilia to its maiden win after just 18 races in its new era of Superbike (the last time the Italian manufacturer won a race was Imola 2001 with the twin-cylinder RSV ridden by Laconi).

## RACE 2

No confirmation was needed but the Brno races proved that Ben Spies was a rider capable not only of riding at the top of his game but also of administering the situation while under pressure. Racing at close range with Max Biaggi looking and trying to pass you at every corner is not easy, especially considering the quality of the adversary.

The American was now just seven points behind the championship leader Noriyuki Haga, who was the other protagonist of this race (which had lots!), the Japanese star riding through the pain barrier to finish sixth, limiting the damage and postponing to the Nurburgring the head-on clash between the two.

# WSBK Championship

*After being taken out involuntarily by Fabrizio in race 1, Spies (19) took revenge by winning race 2. Ten Kate Honda riders, Checa (7) and Rea (65), both got onto the podium in race 1, while Corser (11) took his BMW to fifth place.*

Fabrizio in race 2 rode well and only had the race 1 error that could have hauled him right into the thick of the title battle to recriminate about. Instead he was now 53 points behind the leader and 46 behind Spies.

These three made all the difference on the day, and so did their bikes: the awesome Ducati twins, the simply perfect Yamaha and the rapidly improving Aprilia, which was now at the same level as the others.

The other teams and manufacturers were only able to watch from afar this battle for supremacy but the next round at the Nurburgring was sure to produce some surprises, such as the return of the Hondas, which were somewhat under tone at Brno, and above all the confirmation of the BMW, which Corser was able to take to the front thanks to a new engine tested at Imola at the start of July.

Jonathan Rea took a fourth place confirming he was the best Honda rider out there, ahead of Checa. Behind Haga, who was sixth, could be found Tom Sykes who involuntarily was giving even more prestige to Spies' performances: with an identical bike to the Texan, rookie Sykes could only finish seventh ahead of privateers Byrne and Smrz.

The situation in the points table now saw Haga in the lead from Spies, but by just seven points (326 to 319) and Fabrizio third on 273.

sterilgarda
alimenti
Sponsor del Benessere
YAMAHA
YAMALUBE
FIMER
NGK

65
HANNspree
ids
HONDA
Hanns.G

# (06.09)
# Nürburgring (GER)

Everyone expected Superpole to go to Spies but the American started from row 2, leaving his two chief title rivals on the front row.
Pole position instead went to Nori Haga, the only man to have got close to the track record and he would be flanked by Jonathan Rea and Leon Haslam with the two Hondas; Michel Fabrizio completed the front row.

## RACE 1

The first race got off to a bad start following a lap 1 incident involving Parkes, Tamada and Hopkins (as well as Iannuzzo) that forced Race Direction to bring out the red flags. Hopkins and Tamada were taken to the Medical Centre for checks and then to hospital: concussion for the American and his season was over.

On the restart Haga was quickest off the mark and he immediately gained a few metres on Rea, Spies, Corser, Biaggi, Fabrizio and all the rest. Jonathan Rea was on top form and tried to catch Haga, all the while shadowed by Spies and an incredible Corser, who was right on the American's rear exhausts. At the end of lap 3 Rea was right behind Haga.

On lap 5 Haga again had a lead of around one second but now Spies was on his tail, followed by Rea and then two laps later the American set about reducing the gap to Haga.

At the mid-race point Spies was right with Haga and a battle between these two was on the cards: Jonathan Rea was over two seconds behind. On lap 11 Spies easily slipped past Haga into the lead but the Ducati rider stayed with him. In the meantime Biaggi had passed Corser and had moved into fifth place.

With a few laps left to run Spies and Haga had a lead of five and a half seconds on the Honda duo of Rea and Checa.

Lap 18 was simply fantastic: Haga tried to pass Spies and succeeded but went wide, allowing the American to get back in front. Both riders were looking ragged and at every corner Haga was trying to pass by putting the Yamaha man under pressure.

At the end of the penultimate lap Spies had a half-second lead on Haga who seemed to be settling for second place. Checa meanwhile had overtaken Rea for the final podium place.

WSBK Races

HANNSpree
ids
65
HANNSpree
ids
7
Hanns.G
xerox
41
DUCATI
BREIL

sterilgarda
19
YAMAHA
FIMER
PARTS EUROPE
xerox
Arai
HJC

# WSBK Championship

**RACE 2**

Haga powered into the lead of race 2 as well, followed this time by Checa and Corser. Spies stayed in the leading group but the real protagonist of the early laps was Jonathan Rea who was spectacularly gaining on the two up at the front. Another Honda, this time the Stiggy version of Haslam, was going well in fifth place. On lap 5 Rea made a determined move on Haga, making contact with his Ducati, which crashed without any consequences, but his race was over.

At this point there were three Hondas in the top 3 places and Spies was in the lead of the points standings. The American then made his move and started lapping half a second quicker than Rea, closing in on Checa and Haslam who were fighting for the runner-up slot.

With a third of the race gone Rea had just a couple of tenths on Haslam, while Checa was third, followed by Spies, who overtook him on lap 9.

Rea set a new lap record at the mid-point of the race as he was trying to get away from Leon Haslam, who in turn was trying to hold off Spies: the Texan was pushing to get as many points as possible.

On lap 13 Ben Spies moved past Checa and set off after Rea, while Biaggi was right on Haslam's tail. At the end of lap 18 Spies was on Rea's rear tyre, but the youngster was unfazed as the American tried to pass him at teh start of the penultimate lap. Despite all the pressure the Honda man held on to the flag to win his second Superbike race from the new points leader, Spies.

At the top therefore it was Spies on 364 points ahead of Haga on 346 and Fabrizio, who was out of contention now, on 289. Rea stayed fourth on 244, 20 points more than Biaggi.

*Rea (65) scored another win at the German track, while race 1 went to Ben Spies (19). Carlos Checa (7) stepped on to the podium together with Haga (41). Biaggi (3) had another good race with the Aprilia.*

### Race 1

| | | | |
|---|---|---|---|
| 1° | B. Spies | (USA - Yamaha) | 39'04"818 |
| | | | 157,737 km/h |
| 2° | N. Haga | (JPN - Ducati) | + 3"850 |
| 3° | C. Checa | (ESP - Honda) | + 6"990 |
| 4° | J. Rea | (GBR - Honda) | + 7"109 |
| 5° | M. Biaggi | (ITA - Aprilia) | +12"825 |

### Race 2

| | | | |
|---|---|---|---|
| 1° | J. Rea | (GBR - Honda) | 39'01"561 |
| | | | 157,956 km/h |
| 2° | B. Spies | (USA - Yamaha) | + 0"786 |
| 3° | C. Checa | (ESP - Honda) | + 4"993 |
| 4° | M. Biaggi | (ITA - Aprilia) | + 8"191 |
| 5° | L. Haslam | (GBR - Honda) | + 10"907 |

WSBK Races

# (27.09) Imola (ITA)

### Race 1

| | | | |
|---|---|---|---|
| 1° | N. Haga | (JPN - Ducati) | 38'32"199 |
| | | | 161,388 km/h |
| 2° | M. Biaggi | (ITA - Aprilia) | + 2"074 |
| 3° | M. Fabrizio | (ITA - Ducati) | + 2"190 |
| 4° | B. Spies | (USA - Yamaha) | + 5"438 |
| 5° | R. Kiyonari | (JPN - Honda) | + 14"470 |

### Race 2

| | | | |
|---|---|---|---|
| 1° | M. Fabrizio | (ITA - Ducati) | 38'23"143 |
| | | | 162,023 km/h |
| 2° | N. Haga | (JPN - Ducati) | + 3"592 |
| 3° | M. Simoncelli | (ITA - Aprilia) | + 6"510 |
| 4° | M. Biaggi | (ITA - Aprilia) | + 7"445 |
| 5° | B. Spies | (USA - Yamaha) | + 14"678 |

*Max Biaggi (3) ran a great race at Imola and was always in the leading positions, here in the battle with Haga (41).*

Michel Fabrizio powered to the first Superpole win of his career with a fantastic time, just five-hundredths of a second quicker than Ben Spies and six quicker than Jonathan Rea, the Northern Ireland youngster once again very determined on this track. Noriyuki Haga completed the front row.

### RACE 1

Biaggi powered away quickest in race 1, while Spies had a bit of a moment when his left foot slipped off the footpeg. Behind Michel Fabrizio was right there but on lap 2 Haga powered past on the inside and set after the leader. Rea was taking a few risks in his efforts to pass Haga, then he slotted in behind the Aprilia and the two Ducatis. Spies completed the group but was keeping well out of trouble. Rea tried an impossible move on lap 3 and almost brought some other riders down with him! Corser (BMW) in the meantime was leading a scrapping group made up of Byrne, Haslam, Smrz and Simoncelli.

Three Italian bikes were in the lead with a third of the race gone, and Fabrizio had now passed Haga for second place and was trying to hustle Biaggi. Simoncelli meanwhile had moved up to sixth place and was chasing down Haslam. On lap 10, after powering past Leon Haslam, Marco Simoncelli crashed out from the race. Behind the leading trio Ben Spies had made up some time and was lapping half-a-second quicker than Biaggi and the others. Haslam was almost ten seconds behind.

On lap 18 Haga moved into the lead and pulled away, and Fabrizio tried to pass Biaggi as well. Spies was getting closer and closer and was looking for at least a podium. On the penultimate lap Fabrizio managed to pass the Aprilia for second place, but at the chicane just metres before the line on the final lap Biaggi, with a beautiful move, passed Fabrizio to take the runner-up slot. Spies finished in fourth place.

### RACE 2

Fabrizio and Haga wanted to avoid being caught in the group and rocketed away at the start of race 2, pulling out a few metres lead on Biaggi, while Spies had a bad start and was in fifth at the end of the opening lap behind Byrne. The American was being followed by the battling Simoncelli and Rea, who had had another 'big' moment.

One third of the way in and Haga had seven-tenths of a second lead over Fabrizio and Biaggi

aprilia
sterilgarda
YAMAHA
Kawasaki

HANNSpree
65
ids
HONDA

MATIC
ES
CAM
AUTO
3
58
RIFLE
CAME

# WSBK Championship

who were engaged in a terrific battle. Marco Simoncelli was now behind them after passing Byrne. At the mid-point Haga was almost a second and a half ahead of Fabrizio, who in turn had 2 seconds advantage over Biaggi; Simoncelli was another two-tenths behind and was beginning to feel the presence of Spies behind him. Byrne was doing an excellent job of keeping the American behind.

On lap 14 there was quite a moment at the final chicane before the finishing line: Simoncelli came in too hard on Biaggi who almost crashed. The man from Rome miraculously stayed upright and Spies just as amazingly managed to avoid Biaggi, ending up on the gravel but luckily without crashing.

The Yamaha rider was also passed by Byrne and after losing concentration he overshot his braking, which took the gap to the leaders to 12 seconds. Then he resumed his race and got back into fifth place once again.

In the last few laps Haga rolled back on the throttle and settled for the runner-up slot, which enabled him to return to the top of the points table, three ahead of Spies. Fabrizio continued his record pace and went on to win by a margin of more than two seconds over his team-mate.

The duel between the two Aprilia riders saw Biaggi trying to make up time on Simoncelli but then he realized that it was better to score points for the championship standings, in which the Italian was fifth, just behind Rea.

The table now saw Haga with 391 points, followed by Spies with 388 and Fabrizio with 330.

*The Imola weekend produced a number of surprises after a false start to allow the track to be cleaned. Marco Simoncelli (58), stand-in rider on the Aprilia, had a fantastic race, which included a determined passing move ... on Biaggi. Rea (65) had a couple of off-road excursions, while Michel Fabrizio took his first 'true' race win.*

WSBK Races

87

Mag

# (04•10)
# ny Cours (FRA)

Ben Spies put things beyond reach of his rivals in Superpole with a sub-1m38s time, almost half-a-second quicker than Jonathan Rea, Michel Fabrizio and Max Biaggi, who made up the rest of the front row.

**RACE 1**

Spies rocketed away into the lead followed by Biaggi who was passed a few corners later by Rea. Haga was right on the pace however and soon moved into fourth. There was a spectacular crash amongst the mid-field runners on lap 3 involving Tom Sykes but luckily without any consequences.

Rea was trying to put Spies under pressure but the American easily held him off. For his part Michel Fabrizio finally overtook Haslam and tried to catch the leading group, which in the meantime had bunched together again. At the end of lap 7 Rea overshot a corner and lost touch with the leaders. The youngster stopped at the end of the pit wall to mull over things with his mechanics but his race was over. Spies now no longer had any pressure from Rea but Haga was trying in every way possible to pass Biaggi in second place. At this point the American was back at the top of the table with a six-point lead over Haga. Fabrizio was fourth but some way behind the leading trio.

At the mid-point Spies had a lead of about a second over the Biaggi-Haga duo, who were unable to reduce the gap despite lapping at the same pace as the American. In the final part of the race Biaggi and Haga were continuing their battle, until lap 17 when Haga passed the Italian, who made a futile effort to re-pass him. Camier was running quite well in eleventh place on his debut for Aprilia, the BSB champion trying to catch the quartet of riders ahead of him, made up of Kagayama, Corser, Byrne and Smrz. Unfortunately Leon had to retire when his engine broke three laps from the end.

In the final laps Haga was gaining two or three tenths on every lap and with one to go he was right behind Spies. The two swapped positions once but at

# WSBK Championship

*The battle between Spies (19) and Haga (41) in race 1 was exciting, and it finished with a win for the American. Haga made amends in race 2, in which the Yamaha rider paid the price for a wrong tyre choice. Biaggi (3) finished on the podium twice.*

### Race 1

| 1° | B. Spies | (USA - Yamaha) | 37'57"110 |
|---|---|---|---|
|  |  |  | 160,392 km/h |
| 2° | N. Haga | (JPN - Ducati) | + 0"181 |
| 3° | M. Biaggi | (ITA - Aprilia) | + 5"009 |
| 4° | M. Fabrizio | (ITA - Ducati) | + 16"347 |
| 5° | L. Haslam | (GBR - Honda) | + 22"622 |

### Race 2

| 1° | N. Haga | (JPN - Ducati) | 38'00"282 |
|---|---|---|---|
|  |  |  | 160,169 km/h |
| 2° | M. Biaggi | (ITA - Aprilia) | + 1"480 |
| 3° | J. Rea | (GBR - Honda) | + 6"024 |
| 4° | B. Spies | (USA - Yamaha) | + 18"135 |
| 5° | L. Haslam | (GBR - Honda) | + 21"236 |

the flag it was the American who crossed the line first, a fraction ahead of Haga. Third place went to Biaggi, who was now fourth in the points, ahead of Fabrizio in a distant fourth.

## RACE 2

Biaggi powered away to lead at the start of race 2 but after just a few corners was passed by Haga who started to pull away. The man from Rome didn't give up however and on lap 4 tried to get back in front but Haga held him off. Michel Fabrizio ended up on the ground while running seventh and remounted in last place, while Sykes also crashed for the second time in two races.

Meanwhile Haga continued in the lead but he was being hassled by Jonathan Rea who in the meantime had passed Biaggi, while Spies was in fourth.

A third of the way into the race Rea was able to get past Haga in certain parts of the track but the Ducati man immediately re-took him. All eyes were now on Biaggi who was back amongst the front runners while Spies was losing out in the second split and his gap from Haga was clearly increasing.

Biaggi capitalized on a contact with Rea to move into second place behind Haga who had a clear lead.

Ten Kate Honda's British rider was not giving up however and he was ready to take advantage of any eventual mistake from the Aprilia man.

The last few laps did not produce any more surprises as the top 3 settled for their positions and Spies finished in fourth place, but some way down on the leaders.

YAMAHA

SBK
aprilia
xerox
HONDA

3
HANNspree
65
ids
xerox
41
DUCATI

# (25.10)
# Portimão (POR)

Ben Spies took the pole for the championship decider at Portimao with a fantastic time that was almost one second quicker than Troy Bayliss's 2008 record. For the American it was the eleventh Superpole of the season in 14 races.

Alongside on the front row were Shane Byrne (Sterilgarda Ducati) and Michel Fabrizio (Ducati Xerox), with Jonathan Rea taking the fourth slot for Hannspree Ten Kate Honda.

Noriyuki Haga instead would start from row 3 after not making it into the final Superpole shoot-out run.

### RACE 1

Spies rocketed away at the start and at the end of lap 1 had eight-tenths of a second lead on Biaggi, who was controlling Byrne and Rea. Haga was in seventh place, behind Haslam and Nieto. On lap 5, Spies was still in the lead, with Biaggi three-tenths behind, while Haga managed to pass Nieto, not without some difficulty, to move into fifth thanks also to Haslam going wide. Fabrizio was right in Haga's shadow, protecting his team-mate who looked to be in some difficulty. But on lap 7 there was a sensational development when Haga crashed and the championship title he had in his pocket half-way through the season now looked to be slipping away. A third of the way through the race attention was focused on the battle between Spies and Biaggi: the gap between the two varied from four to eight tenths of a second depending on which part of the circuit they were on. Fabrizio, now free from any team strategy, set a new lap record, while Rea and Byrne were gaining on Spies and looked to be in a position to catch him and Biaggi.

On lap 16 of 22 Biaggi overshot under pressure from Rea, and the Irishman moved into second place. His aim was now Spies, but the Texan was comfortably in the lead up at the front. A couple of laps later Biaggi passed Rea on the straight and moved back into second, while Spies now had a lead of two seconds. On the penultimate lap, Jonathan Rea again passed Biaggi, who was now being hassled by Byrne for third.

So Spies went on to win the first race by two seconds from Rea, who finished ahead of Biaggi and Byrne. Fabrizio finished fifth, but some way behind, followed by Camier, who managed to stay ahead of Checa and Xaus.

### Race 1

| | | | |
|---|---|---|---|
| 1. | B. Spies | (USA - Yamaha) | 38'15"390 |
| | | | 158,442 km/h |
| 2. | J. Rea | (GBR - Honda) | + 1"697 |
| 3. | M. Biaggi | (ITA - Aprilia) | + 2"113 |
| 4. | S. Byrne | (GBR - Ducati) | + 2"757 |
| 5. | M. Fabrizio | (ITA - Ducati) | + 14"753 |

### Race 2

| | | | |
|---|---|---|---|
| 1 | M. Fabrizio | (ITA - Ducati) | 38'19"654 |
| | | | 158,148 km/h |
| 2. | N. Haga | (JPN - Ducati) | + 1"195 |
| 3. | J. Rea | (GBR - Honda) | + 1"494 |
| 4. | S. Byrne | (GBR - Ducati) | + 5"553 |
| 5. | B. Spies | (USA - Yamaha) | + 5"842 |

*Ben Spies sprays champagne over Michel Fabrizio. These two won a race apiece in Portugal but the American, with his fifth place in race 2, was crowned 2009 Superbike World Champion. For the Italian, the win in Portugal was his third of the season.*

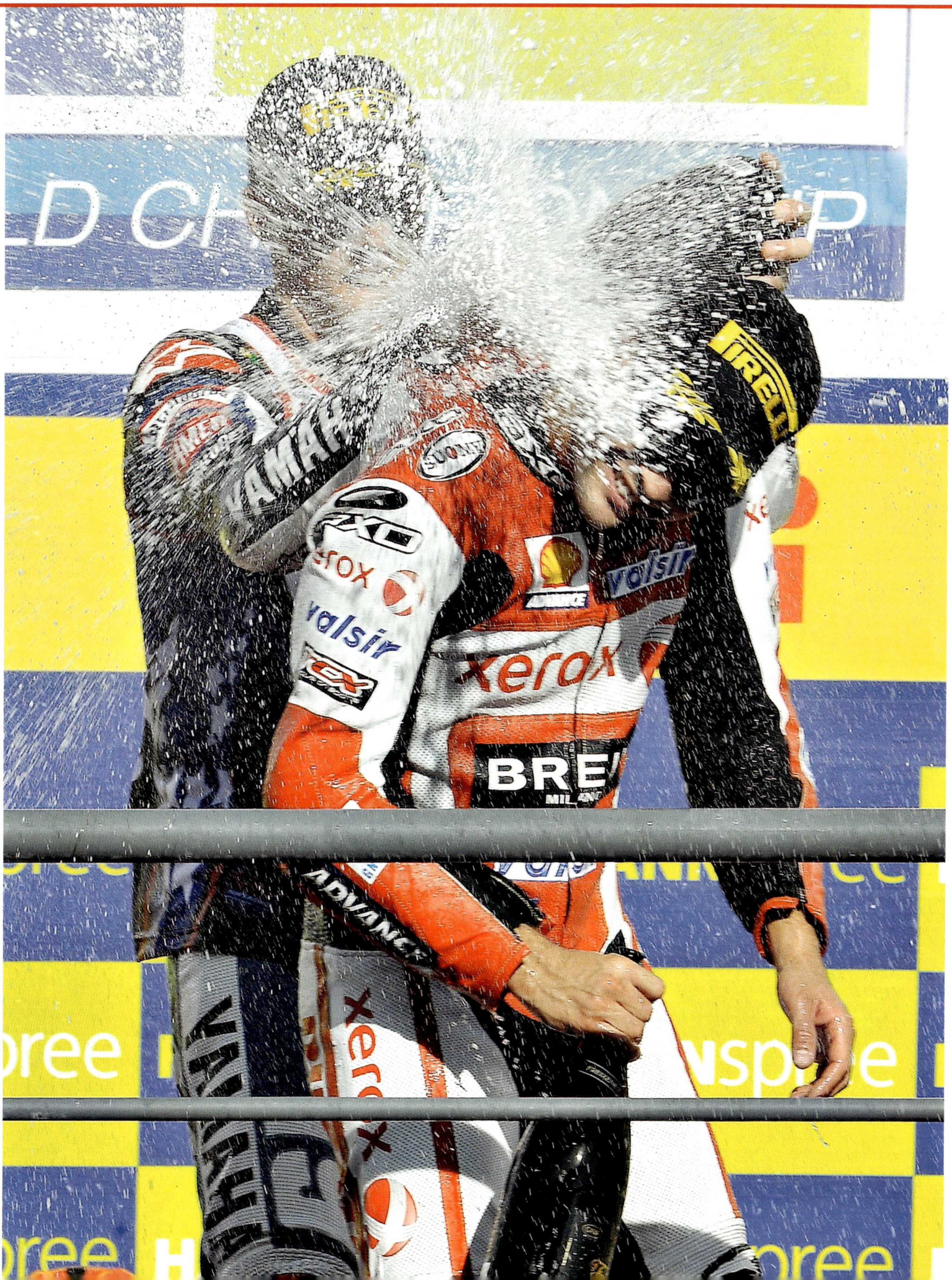
YAMAHA
xerox
valsir
PIRELLI

# WSBK Championship

*Shane Byrne (67) finished the 2009 season in the best possible way with two fourth places on the Sterilgarda Ducati. Two podiums instead for Jonathan Rea (65) who confirmed himself to be one of the best 'rookies' of the season. Biaggi (3) had a competitive weekend, the Italian stepping onto the podium in race 1 and then battling with Spies (19) in the second. Haga (41) crashed out in the first race, which virtually brought the Ducati rider's title challenge to an end.*

## RACE 2

Shane Byrne got the best start, powering into the lead ahead of Spies, Rea and Biaggi. In the early stages the Sterilgarda man headed the field followed by a group of riders made up of Rea, who had passed Spies, Biaggi, Haga, Haslam and Fabrizio.

On lap 4 Rea, who had in the meantime taken over the lead from Byrne, was now up at the front, while Spies was being shadowed by the Xerox pairing of Fabrizio and Haga.

Michel Fabrizio was really motoring and the Roman set a new circuit record, catching up with Byrne and then Rea, while Biaggi was trying at all costs to hold on to the leaders' pace. On the eighth lap, Haga managed to get past Spies and the American was now almost five seconds down on Byrne. Half-way through the race the first three (Rea, Byrne and Fabrizio) were nose to tail with an advantage of two seconds over Max Biaggi, who was controlling Haga (over one second behind). Camier was running well in seventh. On lap 14, Fabrizio passed Rea to move into the lead, while Biaggi latched onto the trio up front, but despite his efforts to keep in touch with the leaders, he was passed by Haga on the next lap. Four laps from the end of the race, Jonathan Rea was back in front again and Haga was right on Byrne's exhausts. Biaggi was fighting with Spies, who was now in fifth place.

On the final lap Fabrizio moved into the lead, and in his attempt to overtake him, Rea went wide and lost his second place to Haga, who missed out on the title by just six points. Byrne finished in fourth place ahead of the 2009 SBK World Champion Ben Spies. Biaggi scored an excellent sixth place, two seconds ahead of his Aprilia team-mate Camier. The Manufacturers' title went to Ducati.

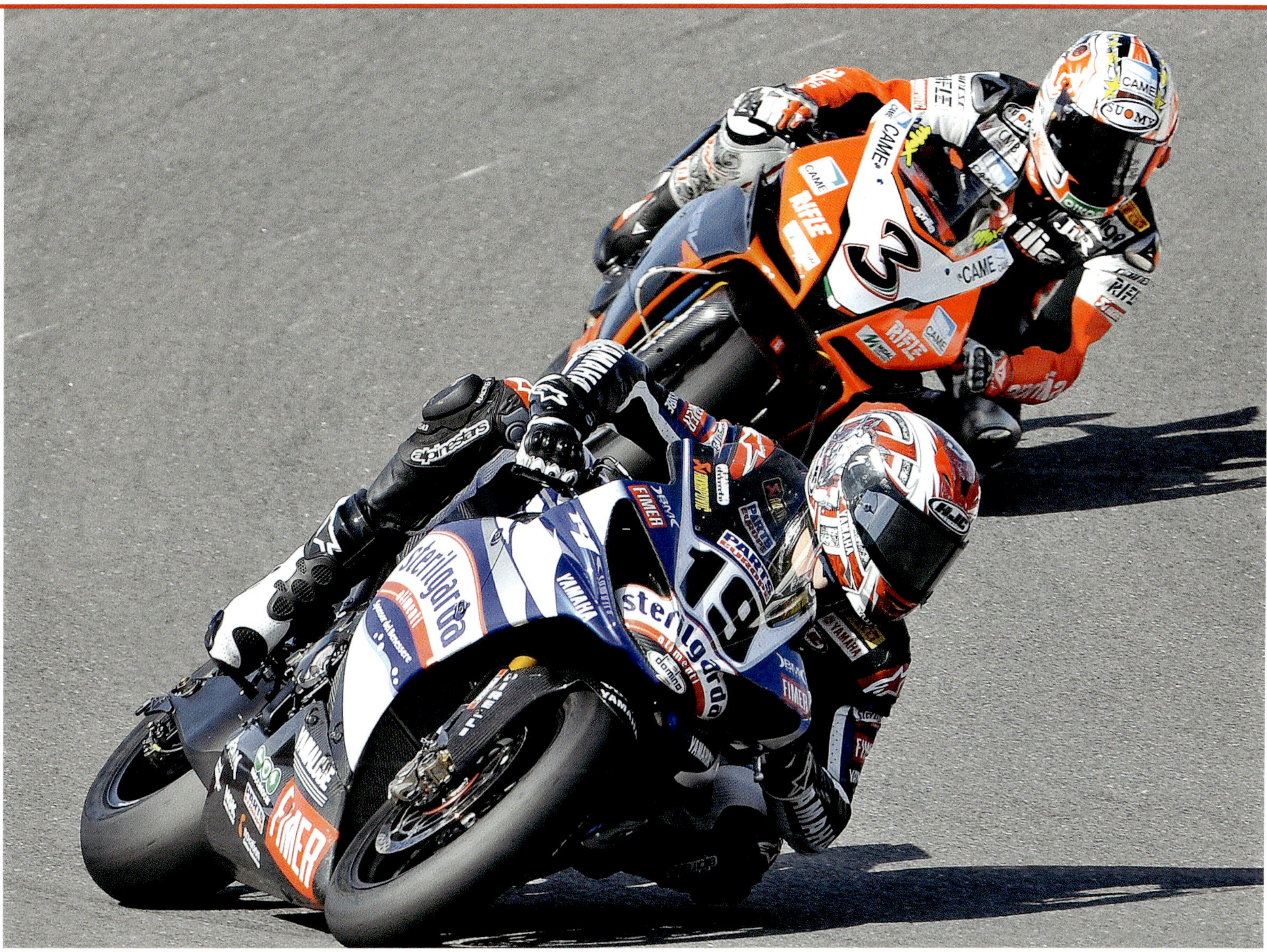

CAME
3
sterilgarda
19
FIMER
YAMAHA


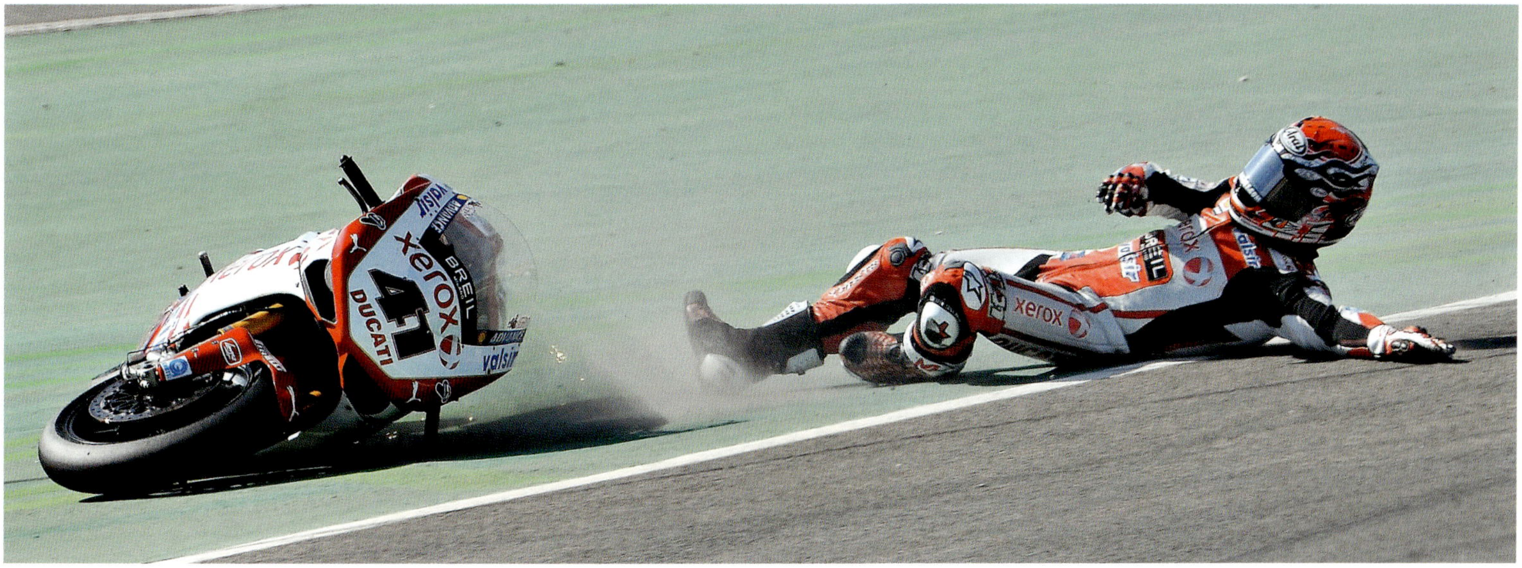

xerox
41
DUCATI
BREIL

Sterilgarda
alimenti
Sponsor del Benessere
YAMAHA
YAMALUBE
FIMER
meccanocar
PARTS EUROPE
NGK
SPARK PLUGS
novation
Carbon Technology
SUOMY
NANKAI
PIRELLI

# Wayne Gardner

## Test

Australia holds a special place in the SBK World Championship. Not only did it, together with the USA, provide the early stimulus for the rise of large-capacity bikes that morphed into modern-day Superbikes, and not only has it been a permanent fixture on the calendar since 1988, it has also produced two title winners and numerous competitive riders.

One man however whose name has never graced the World Superbike stage is Wayne Gardner, the 1987 500 cc World Champion. Infront Motor Sports took the opportunity to invite Wayne down to Portimao to see what WSB was all about, as well as to test the latest factory machinery.

Apart from a brief ride on Kevin Curtain's Kawasaki ZX-10R machine, the last time Wayne had ridden a Superbike was in 1992 at the Suzuka 8 Hours so as tester for Australian monthly magazine Rapid Bikes, he relished the opportunity to get to grips with the bikes. We caught up with him after an exhausting day's testing, just before he headed to the airport for the long trip home to Australia...

"First of all it's an honour and a pleasure to be here, it's my first time to the circuit and it's been a long time since I've ridden such good bikes. The tests have been interesting, I've ridden the weakest ones to the strongest ones, some have a long way to go and some have surprised me the way they are as good as or even better than my GP bikes from the 80s and the early 90s. That's how far street bikes have come in such a short period." When pressed on his preferences of the seven factory machines, Wayne finally came clean.

"Testing all these bikes is like having seven different wives in one day, they've all got different personalities and characters, down to some of the weaker ones that were quite a handful to hang on to."

"The Aprilia was the best bike, it's a very precise, 'point and squirt', and has good power. It was not the

# Test

fastest but it had the most directional, confidence-inspiring chassis, and gives good feedback for the tyres on the road."

"And just behind the Aprilia was the BMW! It steers very precisely and very well, considering it's got a cross-the-frame four-cylinder engine. Out of all the four-cylinder bikes, I'd say this and the Honda were the best handling of the four."

"On this up and down circuit, one of the best bikes around here is the Ducati, I had lots of fun with it. It's got lots of big Vee-twin power, but it's tractable power and the bike was really fun to ride."

"The Honda is always fast and very good. The gearbox felt smooth and precise via the quickshifter. Speed on the straight is good and acceleration is also very strong. With over 215-horsepower on hand, I'd forgotten how much fun a fast race bike was… "

"The Kawasaki was the big surprise, it was right up there! It gave me one of the best lap times and was very confidence-inspiring but their traction control is too strong. I'd say if they fix that up it will be a strong bike next year."

"Probably the Suzuki is one of the weakest bikes out there. It feels big and old-fashioned. It had a great engine but the chassis is a bit outdated, I think the Japanese have got some work to do there to be a front-runner."

"For me the big surprise was the Yamaha, I was expecting a lot more of it. It's probably got the best engine, but the effort required to get that bike around the corner surprised me. It really emphasizes how good Ben Spies is, I believe he's won not on the best bike so it's a testament of his ability."

We then asked him about what he thought of the riders he had seen out on the track on Sunday.

"Spies is an interesting case. He's a lot more technical-minded than I was expecting, he understands exactly what's happening on the bike. For Ben to come into the championship and win it like that is very important. I'll be watching him with interest."

"Rea is a real talent, he makes time in the right places and has a good head on his shoulders for such a young kid. I think he's got a good chance of being a world champion next year, but I hope he doesn't hang around here for too long as he's too good."

"Fabrizio is very fast and very talented but is a bit hot-headed, he needs to have a cold shower on his decisions. He's good but needs to use a bit more brain power on some of the silly moves he's made. He's someone to watch in the future."

We also asked Wayne what he thought of the championship. Despite the fact that his career was forged before World Superbike started in 1988, he has a keen eye for what makes racers and championships tick.

"This is a great class of racing. The average consumer that goes and buys a motorcycle can come and see his bike race, that's the great beauty. It's good advertising for the manufacturers so that's why they show strong support. Because they're all modified street bikes it produces very close racing. There are not just one or two winners, as it is in GP sometimes and there's a great a variety of manufacturers so it puts on a good show on the racetrack which is our stage. TV enhances that and I think that Infront Motor Sports and the SBK championship is really flourishing and has a very bright future. For me it opened my eyes up here how good and professional it is and it was a pleasure to be here this weekend."

Test 99

# Superbike Technical Analysis
# Technology

**Magnificent Seven**

The second year of basically static World Superbike regulations was hardly a year when little changed - the exact opposite in fact.

In terms of the teams and actual motorcycle models, the only WSB combos that remained unchanged in substance were the Ten Kate/Honda CBR1000RR, and the Ducati Xerox/1198F09. Branded the 1198 on the side of the machine, the homologation was still running based on the original 1198cc 1098R roadbike.

For Yamaha World Superbike there was an all-new YZF-R1, for Suzuki Alstare a new GSX-R1000K9 and for Kawasaki a new Paul Bird Motorsports team from England running the same model of Ninja ZX-10R as before, but with a different point of view.

And of course, there were two whole new machines in WSB, run in full factory guise - the BMW S1000RR and the Aprilia RSV4.

In terms of technology and approaches to the idea of how to go WSB racing from first principles, it was a classic year, one of the best ever.

aprilia
PIRELLI

PIRELLI
BMW Motorrad
Motorsport

HANNspree
ids
Castrol
HONDA

Vent-Axia
ZX-10R
Kawasaki
SUPERCASINO.COM

BRUX
DR.BRUX
SUZUKI
ARROW

YAMAHA
Spies
YAMALUBE
FIMER

racing
aprilia
aprilia RACING
AKRAPOVIC
AFAM
BMC Air Filter
PIRELLI

# Aprilia RSV4 - V Four Victory

The small and purpose-built Aprilia RSV4 racebike got several people in WSB hot under the collar, given its uncompromising design which made it as much racebike as roadbike. It has to be said, in fairness, that this is not in any way a unique happening in Superbike. From the very outset, machines like the Yamaha OW01 or RC30 Honda were specifically built for racing as much as road use, and we suspect Aprilia will sell many more RSV4s than Honda, for example, ever sold RC45s.

In any case, Aprilia, like everyone else, met the FIM's requirements and the RSV4 was inducted to the WSB championship from the first round.

A 65-degree vee-four, the Aprilia came laden with technology, including a fly by wire throttle, variable length inlet trumpets, a cassette style gearbox, a neat counter-balancer shaft, and magnesium engine covers everywhere. Titanium valves also help save weight and raise the rev ceiling, and an Akrapovic titanium exhaust, snaking under and behind the engine, completed the uniqueness of the RSV4.

No one else currently makes a vee-four in WSB, but it seems evident that it is a more than valid configuration to take advantage of current WSB regulations.

The petite vee four machine, small in every way except the riding position (with riders from the diminutive Biaggi to the very tall Leon Camier getting on just fine with it) features chassis tech which has been deliberately designed to look like it has just come off the racing track.

The RSV4 structure uses castings and aluminium pressings and after much experimentation on the rear swingarms, Biaggi's machines swapped to using an under slung rear swingarm design, to get the weight lower, and more importantly, give the increase and decrease in rigidity depending on the plane that cornering forces are exerted in. The latest swingarm was the third generation, all made in house, but the linkage ratios are the same, even if the links are now different.

In street trim the chassis weights only 10kg, but the more race-ready element of the design is its almost infinite adjustability. Everything from headstock angle, ride height, swingarm position and even engine placement can be altered with ease on the RSV4, even as a streetbike. Added to the usual high-end components from Brembo and Öhlins, the RSV4 clearly started out as a racebike in roadbike clothes and got more so as the year went on.

# Technology

*Even the airbox is made with huge attention to detail.*

*Rear view of the Aprilia shows how narrow the bike is for a four cylinder.*

*Variable intake trumpets need an actuator and a sensor to measure movement.*

*Cassette style gearbox shaft sits on top of the one-piece clutch casing, clutch basket sits inside, and clutch plates lie below.*

*GPS position antennae sits under rear seat.*

The biggest improvements during the year was to the electronics and rider aids, and until July the main battle was to make the traction control function properly, no mean feat for a factory with lots of two-stroke experience, but little in the way of electronics knowledge since its four-stroke GP experience ended some time ago.

In July an anti-wheelie system was introduced to handle tracks like Imola and Portimao.

Power has never been a problem for the RSV4, with real power coming in at 9,000rpm, and peak power at 14,500 - limited at 15,000.

With variable trumpets being used from the beginning of the year this aspect was the main early problem, and lots of work had to be spent improving the mapping so it became an advantage, not just a very complex new problem.

Power at the top end was not really improved all year, but mapping and corner exit behaviours certainly were.

The adjustability of the Aprilia was used to its full all year, and getting the chain force angle right was a particular point of focus from track to track.

Tyre sensitivity was less of an issue for Aprilia than some others, using the best available tyres for each track, just like the other top teams.

Technology
105

# BMW S1000RR-From Meister

The importance of the BMW S1000RR joining WSB in 2009 is difficult to overstate, as in terms of ultimate long-term threat to the existing volume manufacturers of Superbike machinery, these three letters may be an equivalent of the American emergency code of 911.

WSB was the obvious place for BMW to prove the credential of its highest performing machine ever, a machine that combines some outwardly conventional technology and high-end components with an electronics and EFI package that is absolutely all its own work.

On the surface, the BMW follows the well-worn trail of an across the frame engine and twin-spar aluminium chassis, but it has its own internal solutions which are all BMW.

On the chassis front a whole pile of different offsets and steering angles were worked through in the off-season, and it delivered improvements. During the year Ruben Xaus started to use the Öhlins factory forks, with Corser preferring the feel of the units used in the early season, much more standard material.

Brembo brakes were used, like most in the WSB paddock.

The BMW electronics system is all its own, and a lot of time was spent on the usual traction control and wheelie control, with the ride-by-wire system optimised along the way.

Germany's finest started out with the old electronic system first developed when BMW looked at racing in GPs, but very soon BMW's WSB squad had made their own system, a more robust one, based on series production values and modernity.

At the start of the project development work was split into teams, one for electronics, one for engine, one for chassis, etc, but as soon as possible those teams started work in the same building, all in the same technical group, working alongside of each other.

The S1000RR went through three different mechanical specifications of highly over square engine in its first year. Rumours of desmo operation of the valve train proved to be untrue, but BMW's own small 'F1-style' cam followers were used to keep the engine small, the reciprocating mass slow, revs high and thus the power high.

With the standard road bike producing a claimed 193bhp, there was not so far for BMW to go

# tour to Meister rennen

RUN
START

GEAR
0
0 rpm
TIME
LAP 0:00.00
BEST
to 31.0°C tw 30.6°C
tp 0.0% suf 0.7mm
ssp 0.0% sur -0.2mm
po 1.00bar pf 2.65bar
L1 1.01a/f dru 14.44°
uba 13.2V L4 1.01a/f

# Technology

to reach well over 200bhp. The racebike started the season with a 14:1 compression ratio, from its 80 x 49.7mm bore and stroke figures.

Shifting problems during hard race use caused some changes to be made to the gearbox in terms of friction reduction.

The swingarm went through three evolutions, in terms of side stiffness and torsional stiffness, and also in the rear suspension linkages, all chasing more traction.

The bike was a claimed 162kg, right on regulation for a four.

In August BMW created a dedicated test team, as the previous method of bringing new material directly to races was proving problematic. Steve Martin was a permanent tester, with others brought in to check new ideas and give a wider range of feedback.

**B**MW tailpiece part of their angular styling, Öhlins suspension and rear swingarm very conventional but very effective.

**S**plit brake lines and pressure sensors on Brembo braking system.

**H**igh clutch and gearbox shows off modern engine architecture of BMW.

**I**ncredibly conventional overall design but also strangely individualistic. The Japanese flavour is unissable.

**B**MW display is all part of their own home-made electronics package. LCD display shows whatever the rider wants.

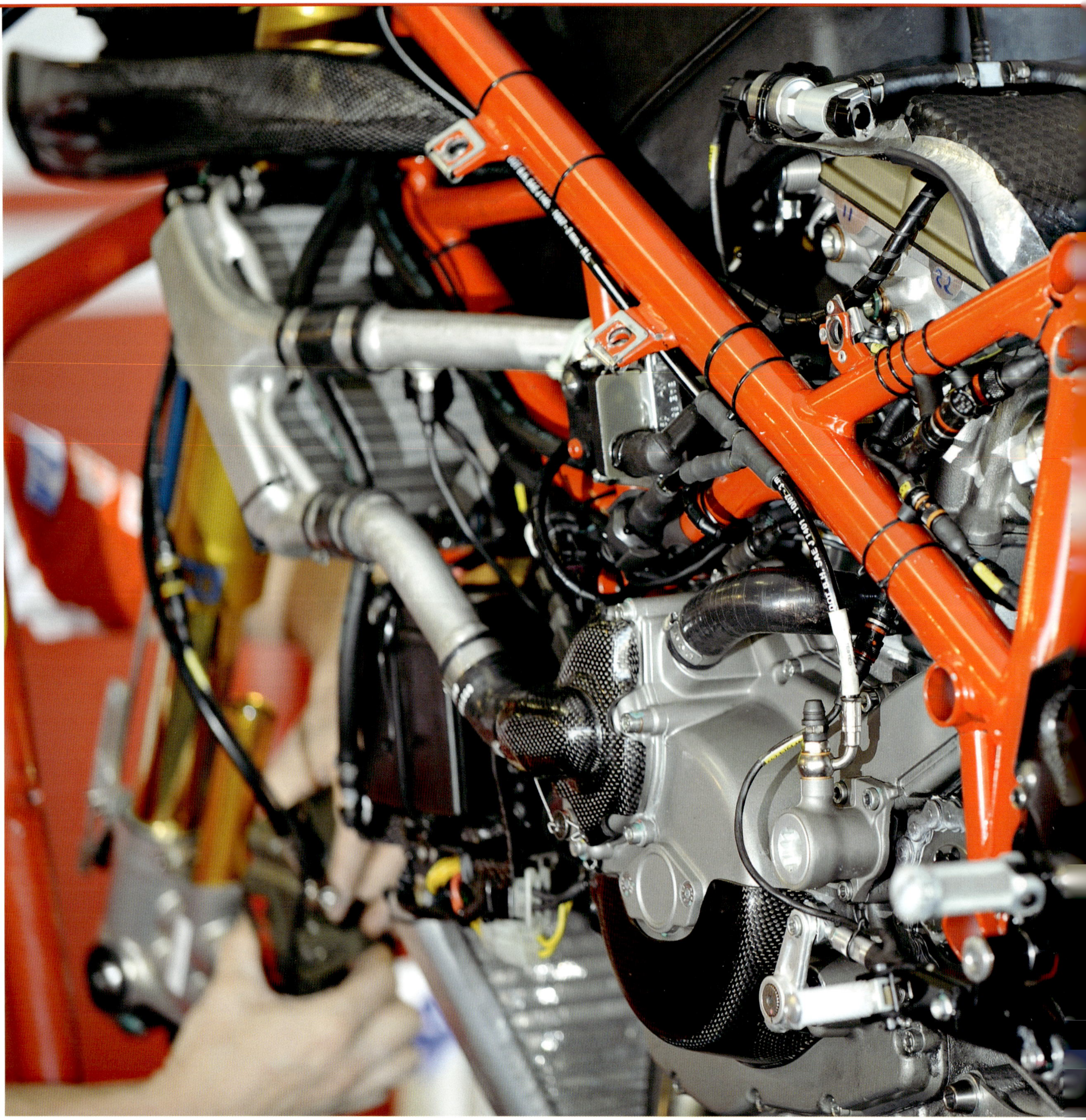

# Ducati 1198F09 - Twin Treat

In terms of steel and alloy parts the 2009 version was little changed. Sure, there were new components here and there, tweaks and changes for reliability and longevity, but given the rev-ceiling demanded by a stock conrod the restrictors plates Ducati hate so much being forced on any user of big twins, there was little point in Ducati chasing too many improvements in internal areas.

On the engine side only work on cams and exhausts were used to change the engine character. At 106 mm x 67.9 mm the engine was largely the same as 2008, but the big change was in the fly-by-wire throttle, only used in the very last race of 2008, but used all the way in 2009. Customer machines did not have this addition, so this was the one thing Ducati really kept in its factory bank. And it made a big difference.

The close relationship with Magneti Marelli continued in the fly-by-wire age, the Marvel four EFI, complete with IWP 162 + IWP 189 twin injectors per cylinder, spitting fuel in measured amounts. With a weight of 168kg, but changeable if FIM handicapping rules dictate it, once more there was no need for expensive options like titanium exhausts, so the Termignoni stainless steel 2-1-2 system only had carbon mufflers to keep the weight of the bike centralised.

Haga preferred a stiffer rear suspension set-up than Fabrizio, but Fabrizio runs more weight on the front than Haga.

Normally Haga uses softer tyres than Fabrizio, generally on the front.

Factory Öhlins TTX suspension running 43mm fork diameters were allied to the almost ubiquitous Brembo brakes, Radial P4X34-38 calliper versions with 320mm discs used each time - just for set-up consistency.

Haga's suspension preferences ensured that he would keep away from the most modern front forks.

The rear swingarm is a Ducati factory part, the same one all year, and it is also now available to buy for race customers.

# Technology

- **L**-shaped 90° vee-twin, belt driven desmo valves, an endlessly competitive motor.
- **H**uge radiator and plumbing dominate side view when body panels come off.
- **W**iring cluster for the Magneti Marelli EFI meets behind digital display Rider's eye view for Fabrizio shows digital rev counter and very flat top triple clamp.
- **E**xhausts are steel, until they meet the carbon silencers.
- **S**ingle-sided swingarm is stronger than stock, and now unique in WSB.

112 Technology

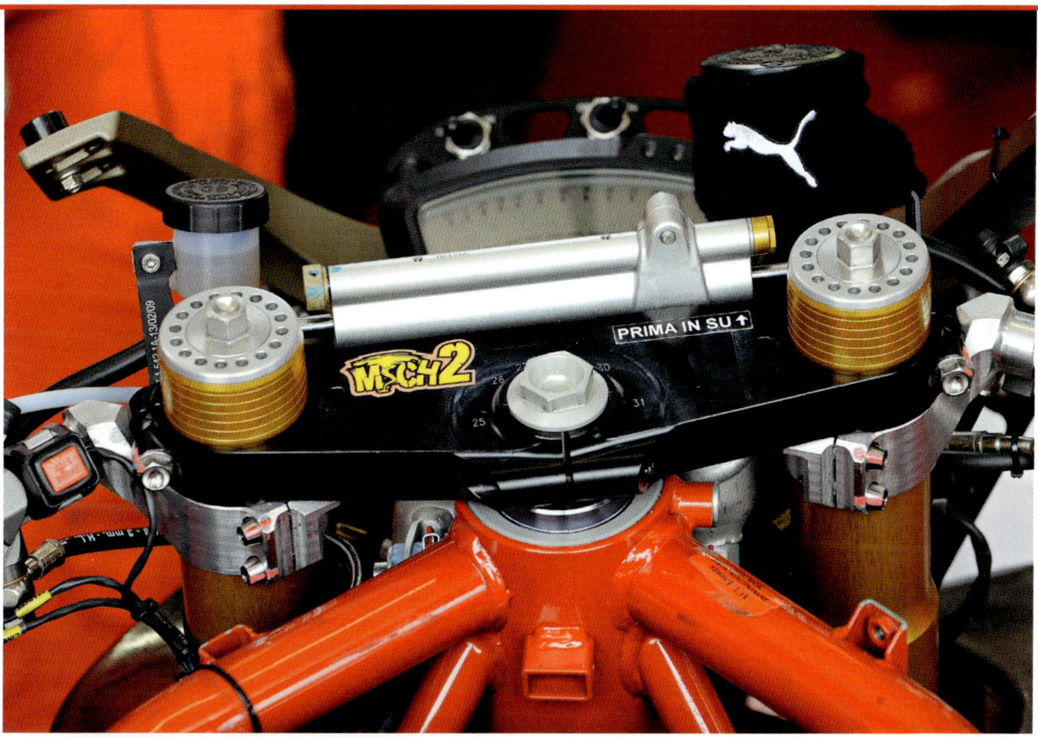
PRIMA IN SU ↑

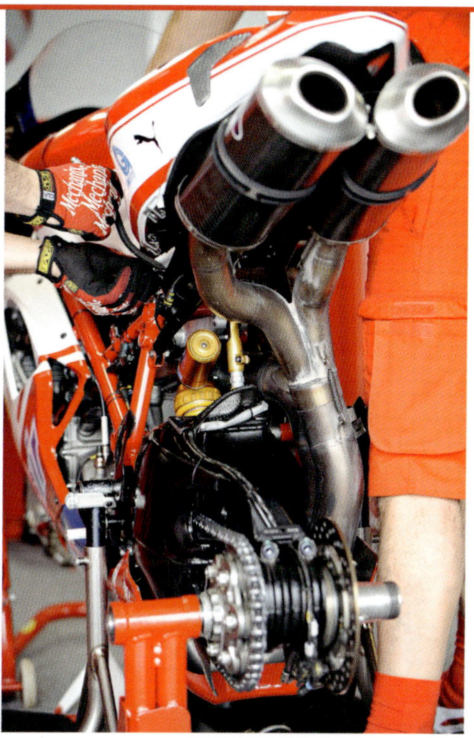

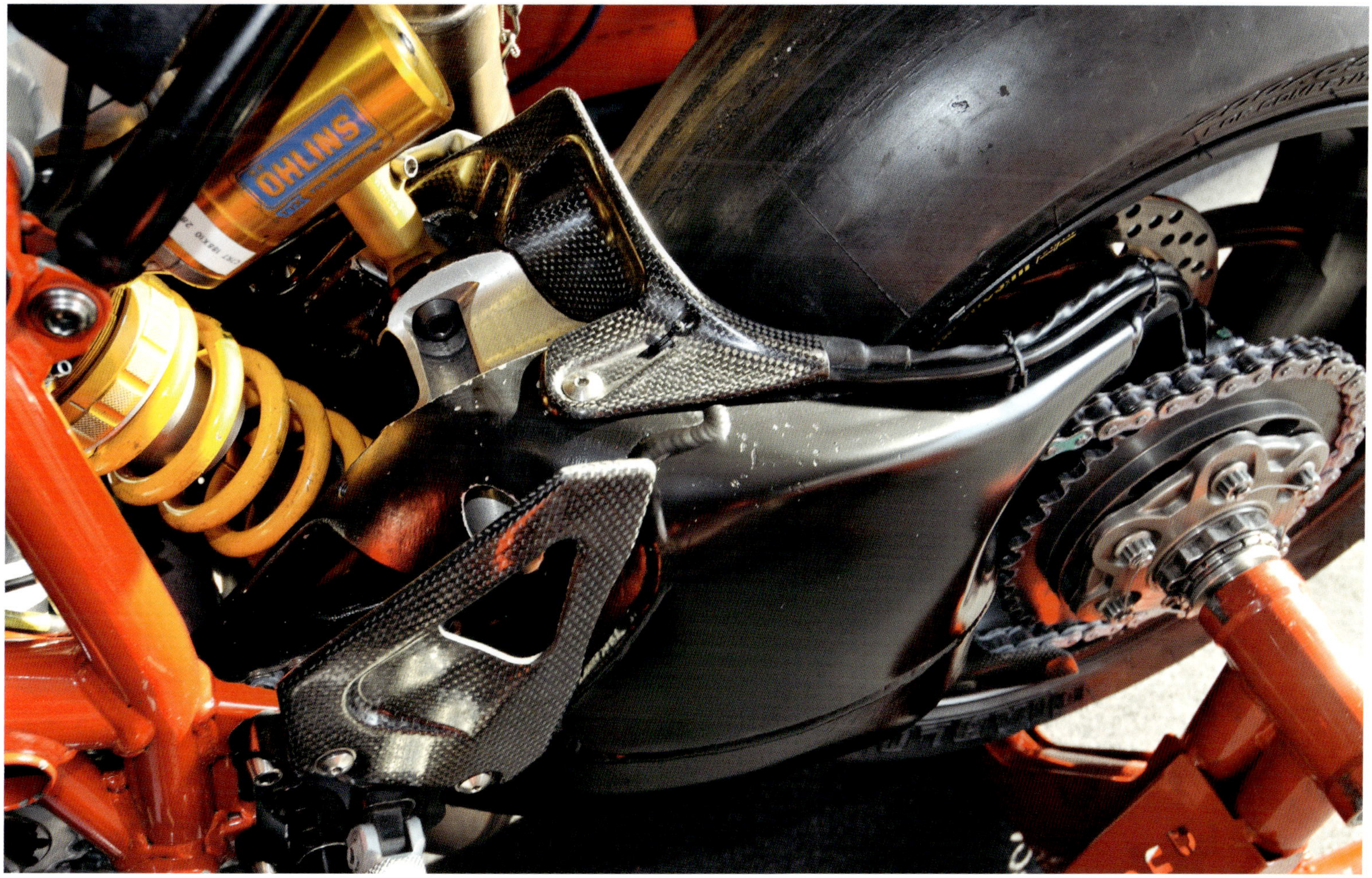
ÖHLINS

# Honda CBR1000RR - More Of

Even the machines that was supposed to change least ended 2009 having major changes in its make-up, partly due to rider preferences inside the team and partly due to a lack of development from some previous technical partners.

Of all the top teams in WSB, Ten Kate value, and make the most of, the technical freedom they have as a privateer effort representing a major manufacturer.

Hence they have always had to combine their on-track experience with their tuning and parts and engine supply business, not only to make it all pay, but to find their own edge in terms of development.

But this year, with three very different riders to keep happy, they sometimes ended up with three different kinds of rear swingarm in the same garage at the same race.

Midway through the year Ten Kate did the unthinkable and changed their suspension supplier from long-term partners WP to the now almost ubiquitous Öhlins. It's difficult to overestimate how important this change was, but with a relative lack of on-site development from WP in the eyes of the team, and results suffering in this intense year, Andreani were called in to look after the new Öhlins from Misano onwards.

Despite this major change in direction, Ten Kate still did most of their own work in-house, including their latest PI Research EFI systems.

With over 215bhp at the rear wheel occasional chatter was largely eradicated by the new suspension, but each rider often had very different machine set-ups.

Rea was a big fan of the KR rear swingarms from the start, but track temperature sensitivity saw Checa go from KR to kit swingers and back again.

On the engine side, there were great pains taken to try and improve the throttle connection, making for a couple of completely unscheduled tests sessions, and at one stage the entire rider aid system was wound down to almost zero for Jonathan Rea, as he felt that the system was actually stealing power from the bike in key areas. The electronics package was thereafter built back up piece by piece as required. This was a major change in development focus even before the first Öhlins units were tried out.

# The Same

HANN

motoholders
ÖHLINS
Andreani
TK11
ARROW
UNIT PRO-LINK
SUNSTAR
DISC POWER
World Braking Scene with
YUTAKA
REGINA
CHAIN
NISSIN
Pro-Bolt
PVM
WHEELS-BRAKES
NGK
motoholders
HONDA

# Technology

Another, and sometimes highly visible change was the Arrow exhausts used by Carlos Checa. In an attempt to make the engine more linear and predictable he opted for longer exhaust cans, but it appeared that eventual software changes, and finally new suspension, were more effective, as the exhaust mods were short-lived.

A complicated and ever-changing 2009 for the Ten Kate team, it did deliver some wins for their Öhlins-equipped bike.

*Öhlins forks; an unthinkable addition to the ten Kate machines at the start of the 2009 season, but they arrived for Misano.*

*Rider inputs to the home-brewed EFI system come via coloured buttons.*

*Black swingarm is kit version, sometimes favoured by Checa, while Rea was more of a fan of the massive KR version. Note stubby exhaust, which Checa had made longer for a while mid-season.*

# Kawasaki Ninja

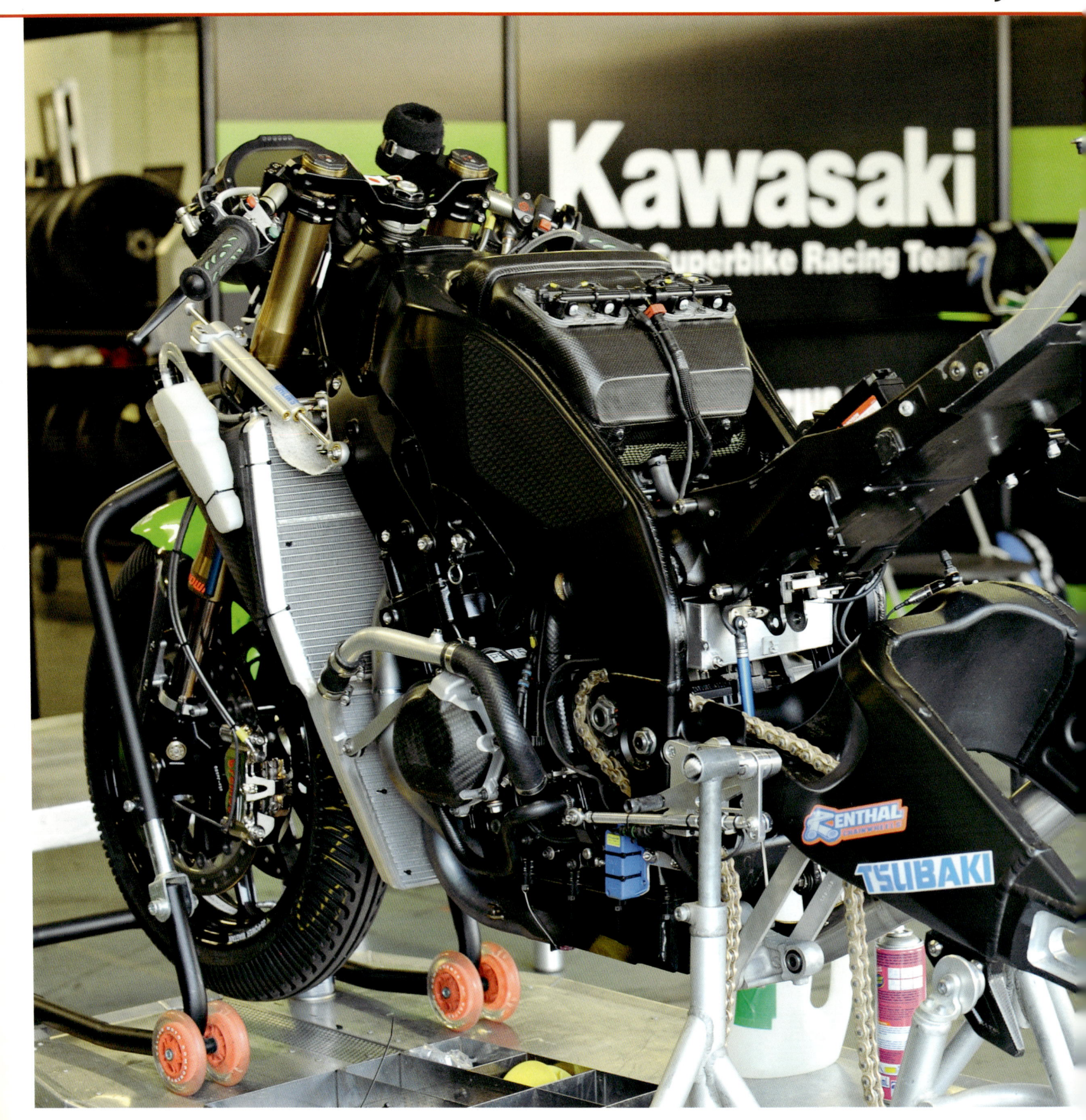

# ZX-10R - Year Two Too Tough

A year older, the basic Ninja ZX-10R was a difficult design to turn into a leading edge World Superbike contender for anyone, and with so many new and improved competitors, top tens were welcome, if few.

The new official Kawasaki team, based in the north of England, had won numerous BSB honours, and even a couple of World Superbike races when running Ducatis.

In their first year as an official partner with Kawasaki, the team started out with one bike largely based on the development line from Japan, and one more home-grown. Hence declaring too much specification for the season, or even for each bike, is an almost impossible task.

The engine was still on the peaky side, but with over 200bhp on tap this was not the major cause for concern.

What was, proved to be its dislike of turning onto corners, a seemingly unsolvable problem, despite several changes of geometry and a new swingarm that got rid of lots of chatter, but not all of it.

Of more importance was a new bracket to hold the engine in a different place, which appeared midseason.

This stiffened the chassis, and being an addition to the frame, was allowed by regulation.

The beautifully made, machined from solid billet rear swingarms were finally fitted to all the machines in the garage, replacing the race kit items, but there were many changes from previous years in terms of other components used.

Factory Showa suspension was at least an attempt to gain an edge, and also Japanese-made Arata exhausts came in a variety of diameters, and some were more tucked-in than others.

Brembo brakes were a conventional choice.

Expect more factory involvement in 2010.

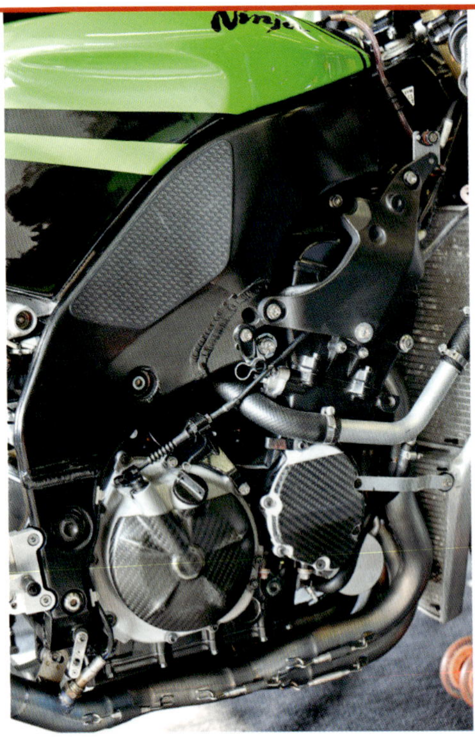

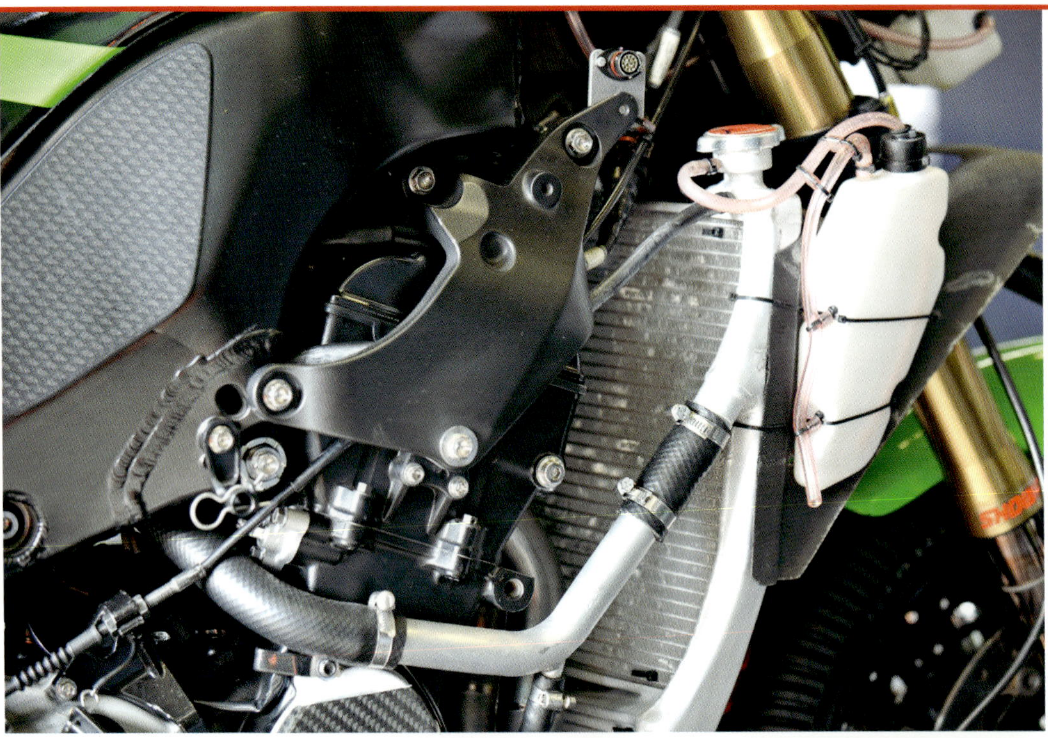

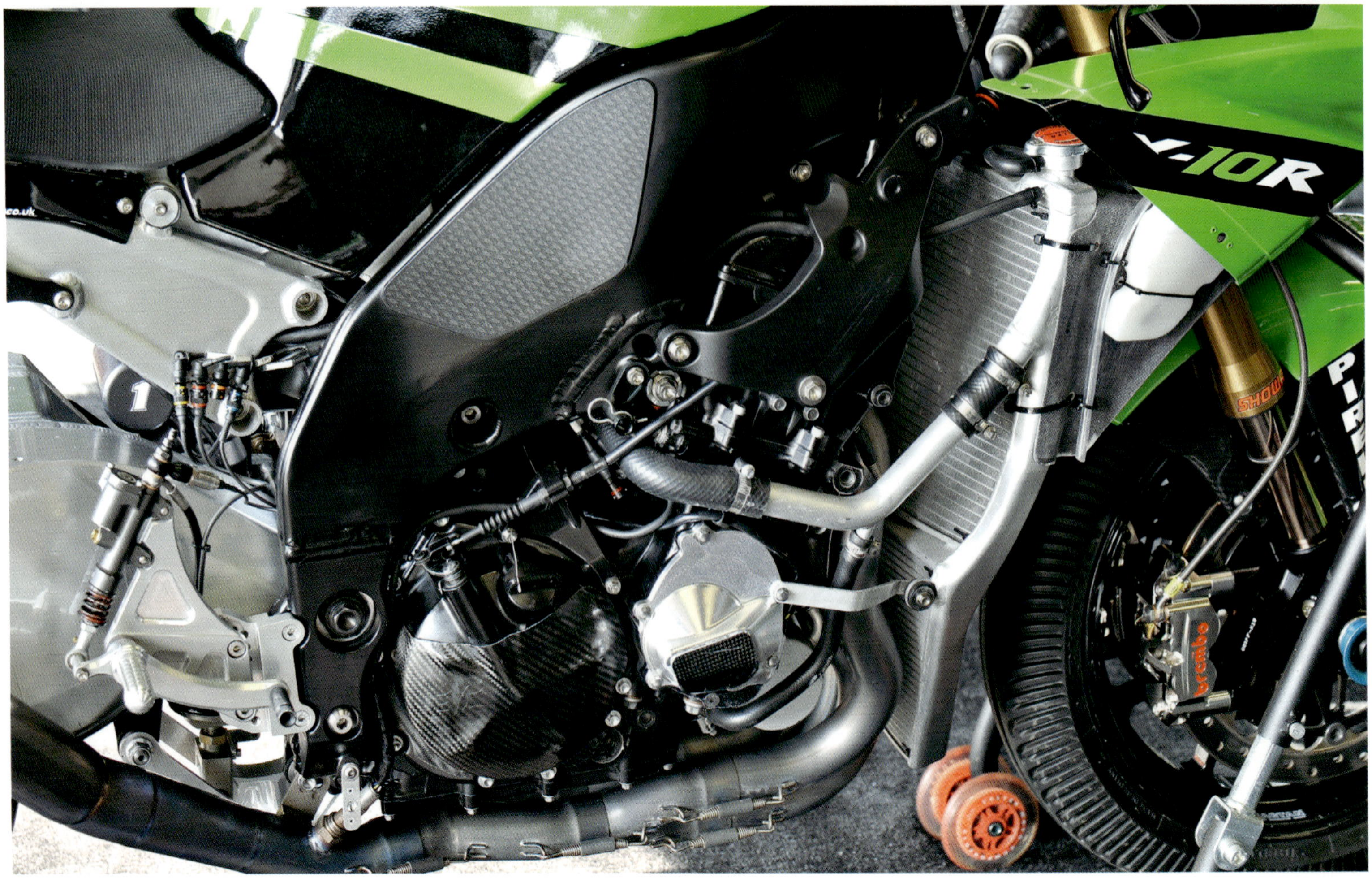

# Technology

**C**hassis grew modified hangers mid-season.

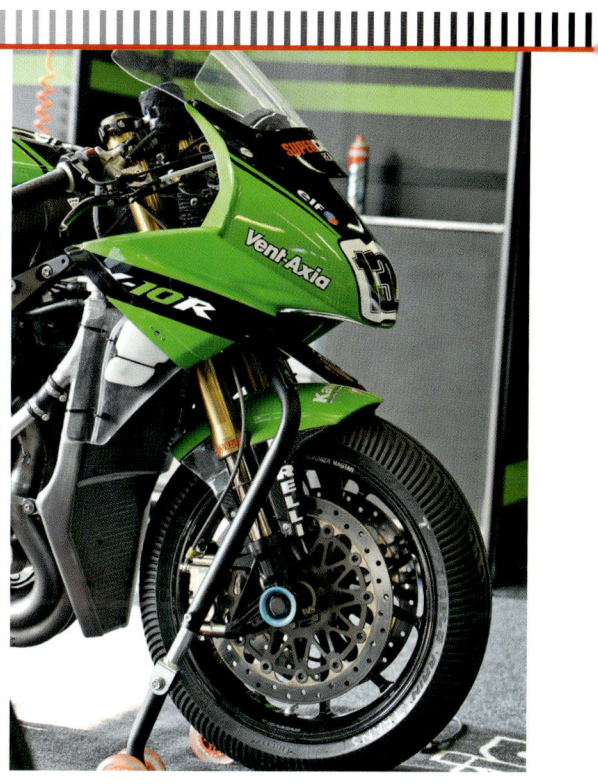

**U**nique Kawasaki chassis design, a sort of up-and-over twin-spar aluminium affair.

**R**ear linkages were changed to help factory Showa suspension and also make corner entry easier.

**S**howa forks became unique in top category after Suzuki went to Öhlins late in the season.

**A**rata exhausts were unique and changed in design as the season went on.

# Suzuki Alstare GSX-R1000K9

The latest in the incredibly long line of GSX-R Suzukis was a definite step into relative modernity, with engine architecture finally obsessing on mass centralisation and reducing overall size.

The result was very much a GSX-R with a more modern gearbox/countershaft/crankshaft relationship, increasingly over square engine and bigger valve sizes than '08.

Sensitivity to track temperatures was not a great point of the 2009 machine, but frequent changes of riders because of injury to Yukio Kagayama and particularly Max Neukirchner were a major problem in terms of marking out a clean development path.

The chassis and swingarm design is all new, including the linkages, and the biggest change over the K8, and it took some time to get a decent set-up. The tyre choices available in the early season did not suit the Suzuki too well, meaning they had to use the softer options more often, in a similar fashion to BMW. Requests to Pirelli brought forth some new tyres, first at a Monza test, and from then on the bike has been easier to set-up, and to find race tyres that last like the rest of the rivals.

A shock change from Showa to Öhlins, after a short tests in Japan, came forth at the end of the year.

The riding position of the new GSX-R is a little higher than in 2008, but the triangle of footpeg, handlebar and seat position is basically the same as before.

Nissin brakes were adopted in the winter thanks to the request of Neukirchner, moving away from the more frequently used Brembos.

The engine gave 212bhp @ 13,300rpm from its 74.5 x 57.3mm bore and stroke engine but in general the team felt this year's engine lost a little in terms of last year's basic characteristics and top power. The team did not stop working on this and even planned new camshafts for the Portimao race.

Big double exhausts on the roadbike were ditched for, firstly, small round versions, with little silencing. Later in the year diamond shaped silencers cans arrived, which matched in with the latest engine development work.

## - New And Unproved

rpm
TIME
LAP 0:00.00
TH 3.0 ST 48.1
WT 74 OT 110
FP 4.8 OP -0.1
TC 1 EB 3
VB 0.0 AD 948

# Technology

*Rear wheels speed rotor was bolted onto sprocket.*

*Incredible conventional Suzuki was made more competitive by engine architecture changes and overall shortening of the machine.*

*Digital dash now more common than 'clocks' and this bike has unique Showa fork top adjusters.*

*Diamond shape rear exhausts came in through the season.*

*Quickshifter incorporated to the gear lever, to new 'high-mount' gearbox.*

# Yamaha World Superbike

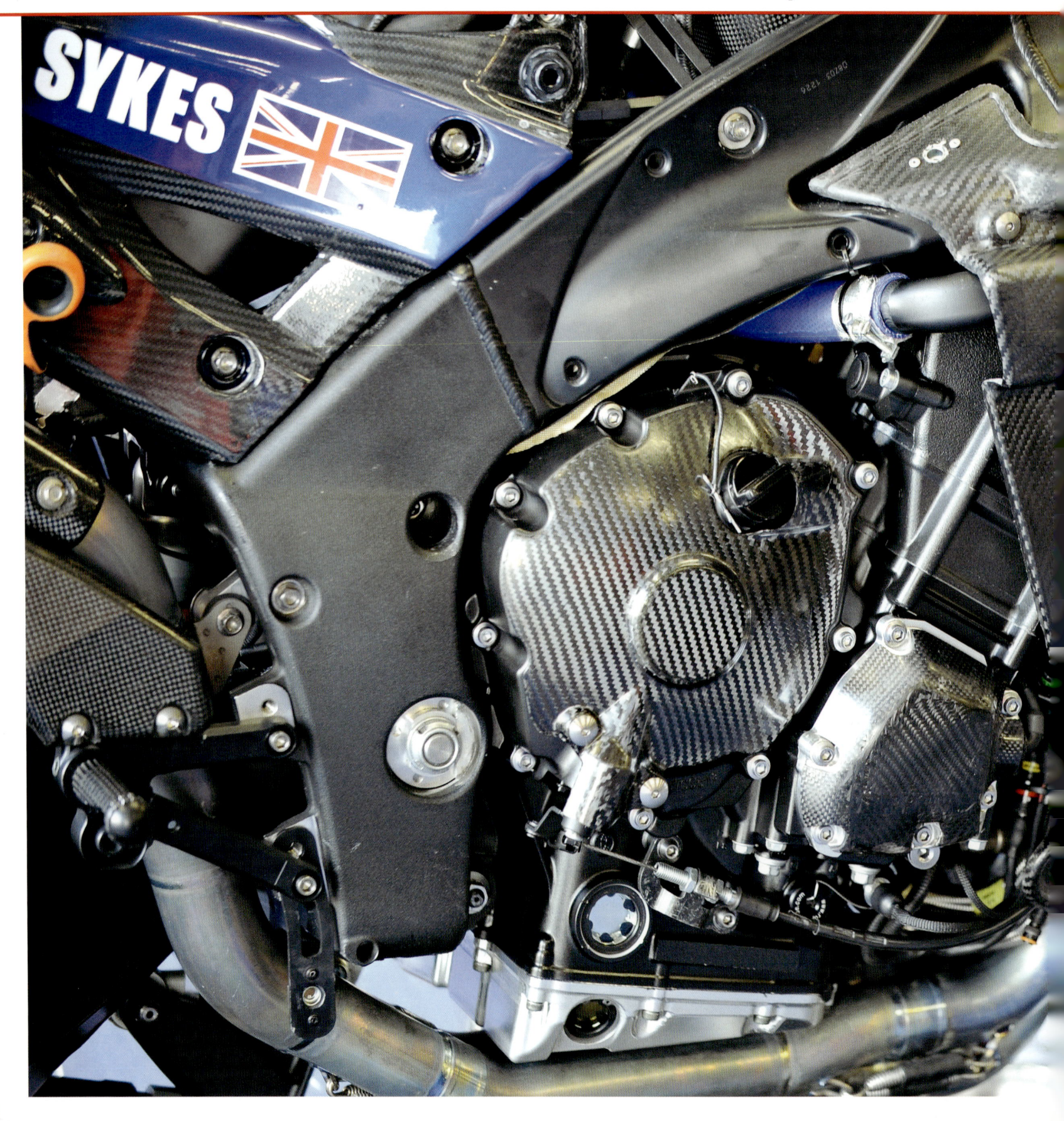

# YZF-R1 - Crossplane Traffic

The best Japanese bike in WSB? Probably. As good as the Ducati or the all-new Aprilia? Apparently not, according to some who would have intimate knowledge of these things.

At the start of the season the unique cross-plane crank on the latest Yamaha R1 was seen as a genuine advantage, allowing the riders not only to get the power down relatively early, but also modify corner lines on a closed throttle, which conventional fours are less than happy doing.

The motor features a crank that fired more like a twin than a four, harmonising combustion torque and inertial torque from the flywheels, which in theory makes the throttle connection far more linear.

The unique Akrapovic 4 into 2 into 1 into 2 exhaust was made in titanium, plus a modified camshaft design helped the R1 to reach a power output over 215bhp in race trim. According to the riders, the machine almost felt slow in terms of the engine performance, until the lap-times were checked.

The engine architecture of 78 x 55.2mm was modern, if unremarkable in this class.

The chassis itself was a changed item from the previous R1, made in several sections, and for WSB use some bracing and gusseting was used to improve the overall package.

Öhlins TTX forks and rear shocks were used; the latest material from the Swedish factory, and this year's new toy was an electronic steering damper, which linked into the Magneti Marelli electronics system. With electronic suspension banned, this was one new area in which Öhlins could experiment.

An under slung custom swingarm, with the 'banana' curving downwards, was voted a success, and some 20% stiffer than the standard unit.

The key to the R1's unique nature was, of course, engine, but the machine really did not stop there in terms of moving in a different direction from most.

The fuel tank was not just under the seat; the fuel filler cap was just the seat, because the whole thing was a form of sub frame that was not really a sub-frame at all, just a big fuel

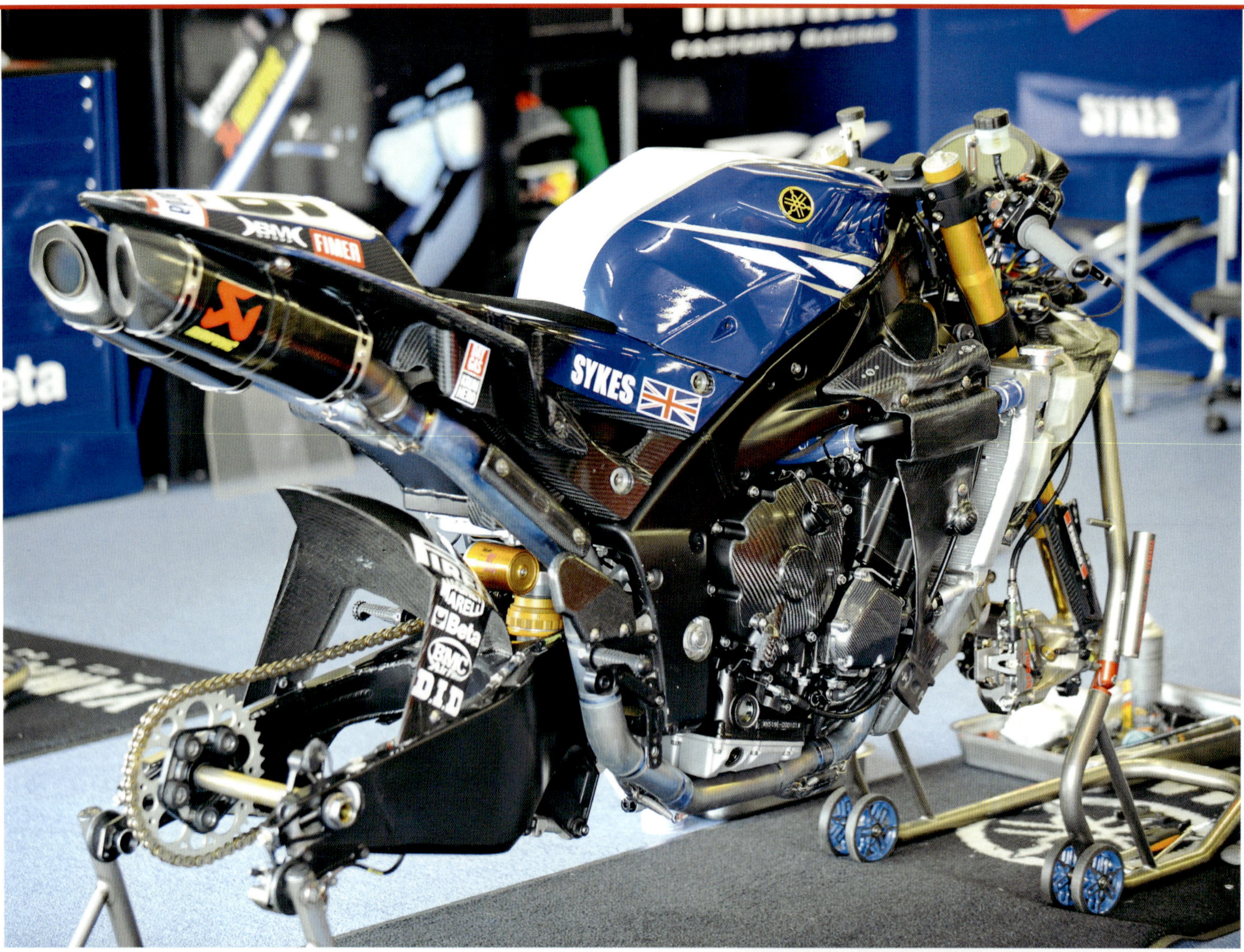

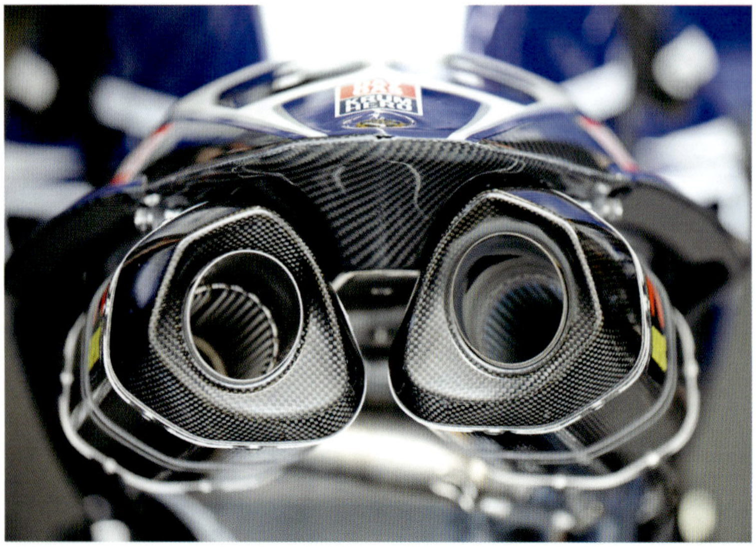

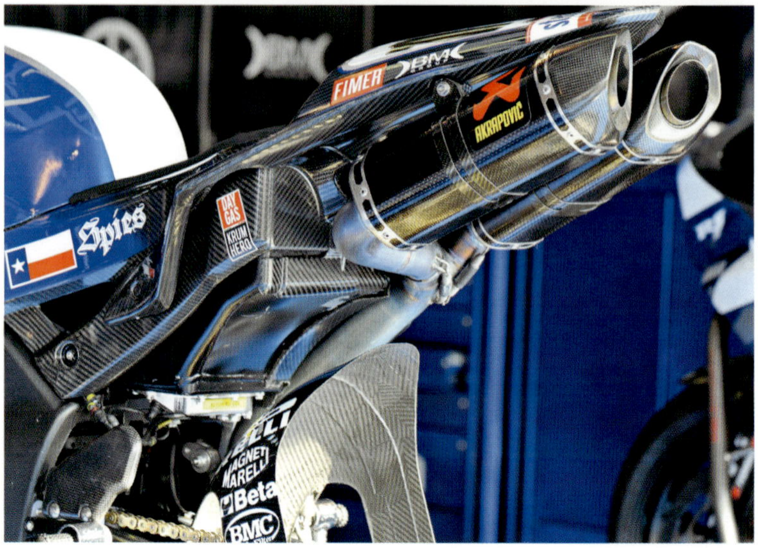

# Technology

tank with bits bolted onto it.

The fuel tank position brought changes in geometry, but the riding position itself was changed from an Imola test onwards, to bring the riders further back and help the bike turn a little better.

The place when the fuel cell would normally sit was taken up by the top of the airbox and most of the electronics package.

In general the R1 was a move forward, but maybe not the leap it was hoped to be. Spies appeared to be the biggest tuning aid of all.

*New Yamaha was denser in build, but still very much R1.*

*Rear exhausts hug the tailpiece.*

*Fuel tank under the seat clearly visible, with sensors on alloy plate underneath it.*

*R1 engine shows little outward sign of its radical interior. Note deep racing sump.*

*Bodywork has to mimic roadbike, but this one even has bulges where headlights would be!*

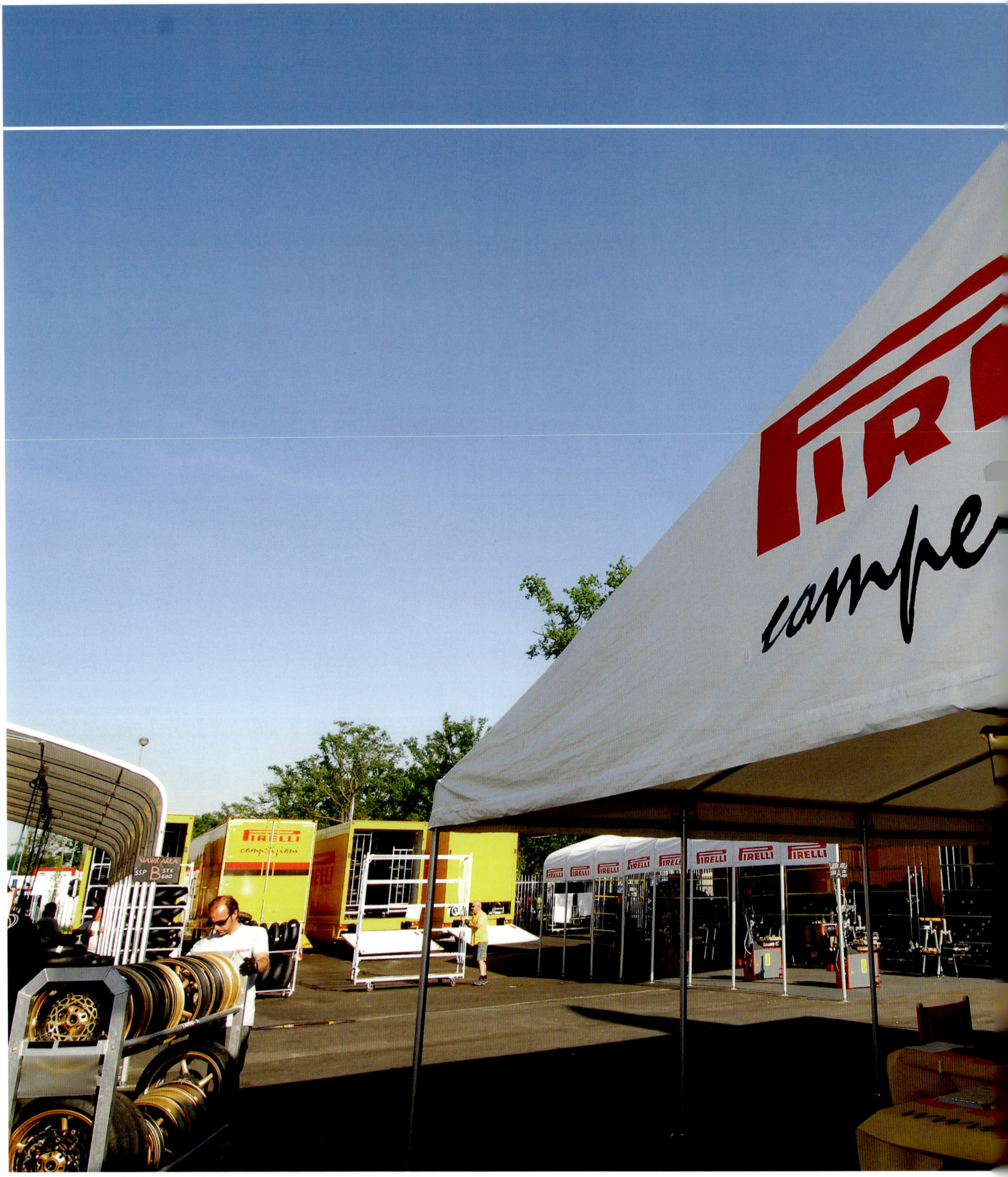
PIRELLI
WORK AREA
SSP B STK 600

## WSBK Championship
# Tyres

The one-make tyre rule was introduced in Superbike in 2004 and it now forms part of the tradition (as well as a great resource) of this category. Infront Motor Sport, at the time called FGSport, adopted the rule in that year and it was a revolution in the world of motorbike racing.

There had previously been other experiences but mainly in minor championships: World Superbike was the first true test-bed in the world for high-performance motorbike tyres.

"There has only been one innovation this season", declared Giorgio Barbier, Pirelli's Superbike Project Manager, "and it concerned the Superpole, which in the new format required longer-lasting tyres. But the real aim was to provide a high-performance product at a competitive price ".

The global panorama has actually witnessed a downturn in the number of people willing to spend any sum of money for a high-performance product. So it was necessary for Pirelli to increase the duration of its product and widen the range of use.

"Yesterday's project was aimed at performance without limits, trying to get all competitors to improve their performance. Today's aim has on the other hand been to flank the performing products with a series of tyres destined for longer use".

"We believe we have achieved this aim", continued Barbier, "seeing as amongst the various types of tyres that we have made available for teams and riders, there have been two (one front and one rear) that have been used by every rider. The most important aspect however is that they went well on every type of bike".

As in every self-respecting company, in Pirelli they also maintain that sport is the ideal environment in which to experiment and then subsequently apply the results to production.

"In fact the concepts applied in tyres used this season will be introduced onto the market in 2010 and these technical guidelines will continue throughout the next season".

# Tyres

*Pirelli supplies tyres to all four Championship classes. The improvement in performance has been notable both in terms of lap time and tyre duration.*

It will be interesting to see the practical applications with the introduction of the standard sizes stipulated in the 2010 technical regulations.

"The 6.25 tyre", says Barbier, "is the maximum size that can logically be used for the rear in normal production. Larger sizes would involve a very expensive modification to the bikes currently on sale. For the front tyre we have proposed (and it was accepted into the regulations) the use of the 3.50, together with what is considered to be its natural evolution, the 3.75. Experience has shown how all the other sizes make a substantially irrelevant change to the performance".

There has been a lot of curiosity surrounding the new Superpole, which has allowed the use of only two 'qualifying' tyres for the three-stage format.

"After an early period of acclimatization the new formula was appreciated by everyone. From a Pirelli point of view the duration of the tyres we made available was a real surprise in that they could be used for 5 or even 6 laps. Some riders even used the same tyre in two different stages of Superpole".

That goes for the 'slick' tyres, what about the 'rain' tyres?

"We also used the Superstock tyres for development", added Barbier. "We did a lot of important work in these categories. For example in Superstock 1000 after adopting a new front tyre at the start of the year, we introduced after just two races a new rear that combined better with the front. In Superstock 600 on the other hand, in the last four races we made a new rear available. Basically we are aiming at improvements in both tyre performance and duration in all categories".

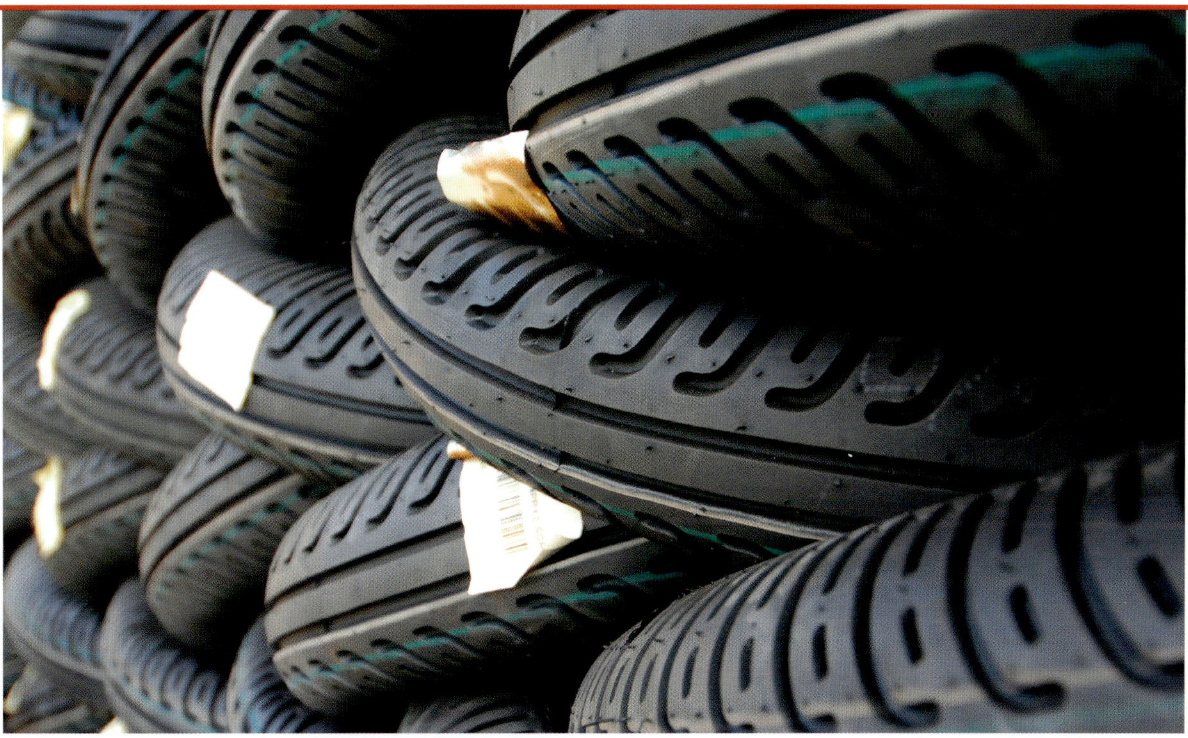

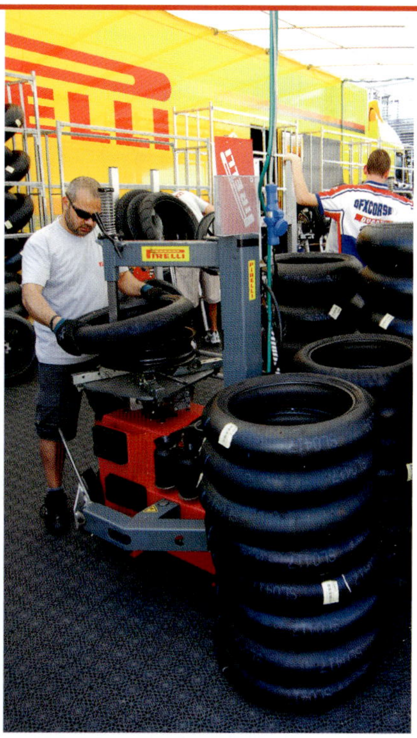

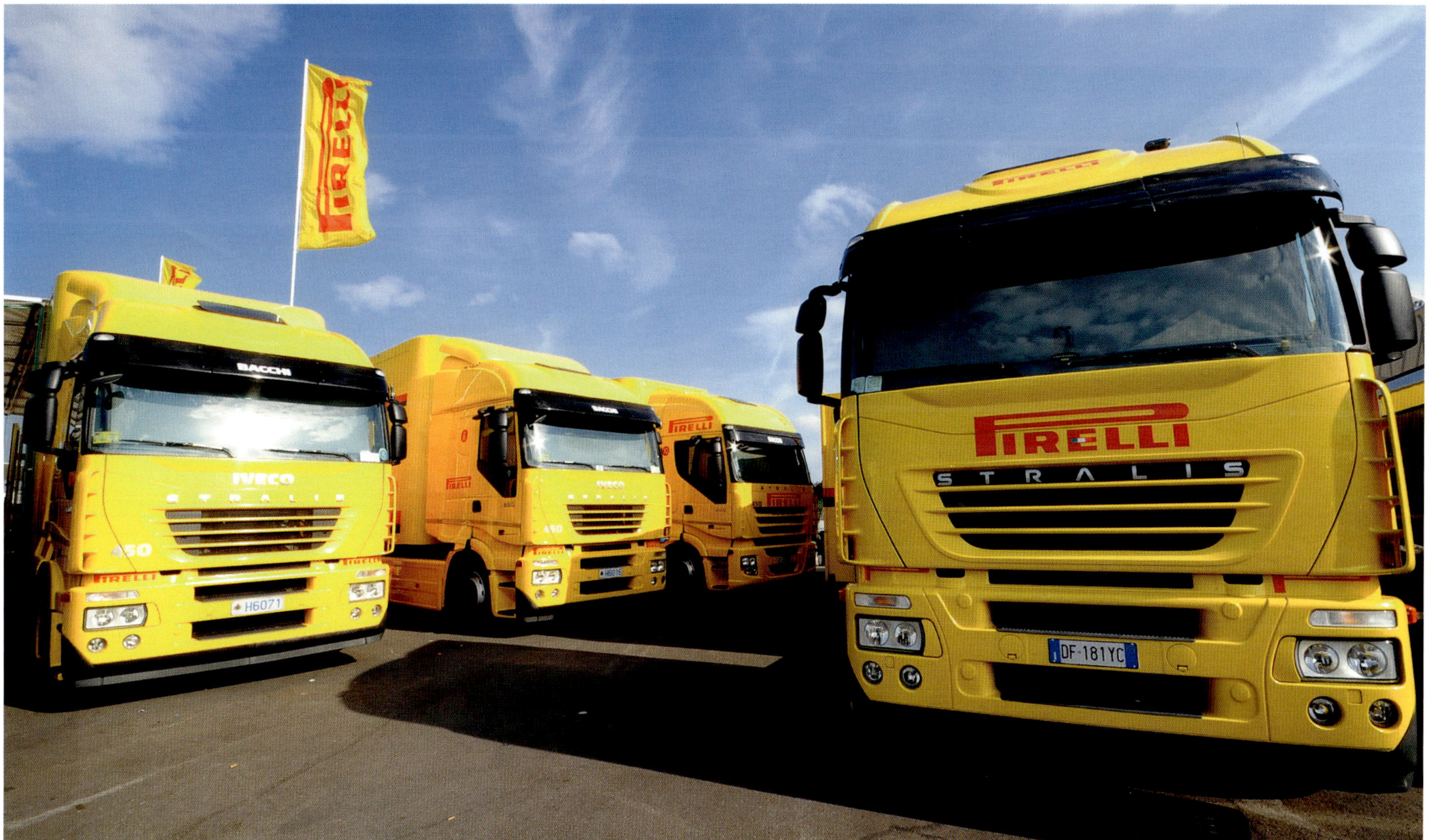
PIRELLI
STRALIS
DF·181YC
IVECO
H6071

## WSS Championship

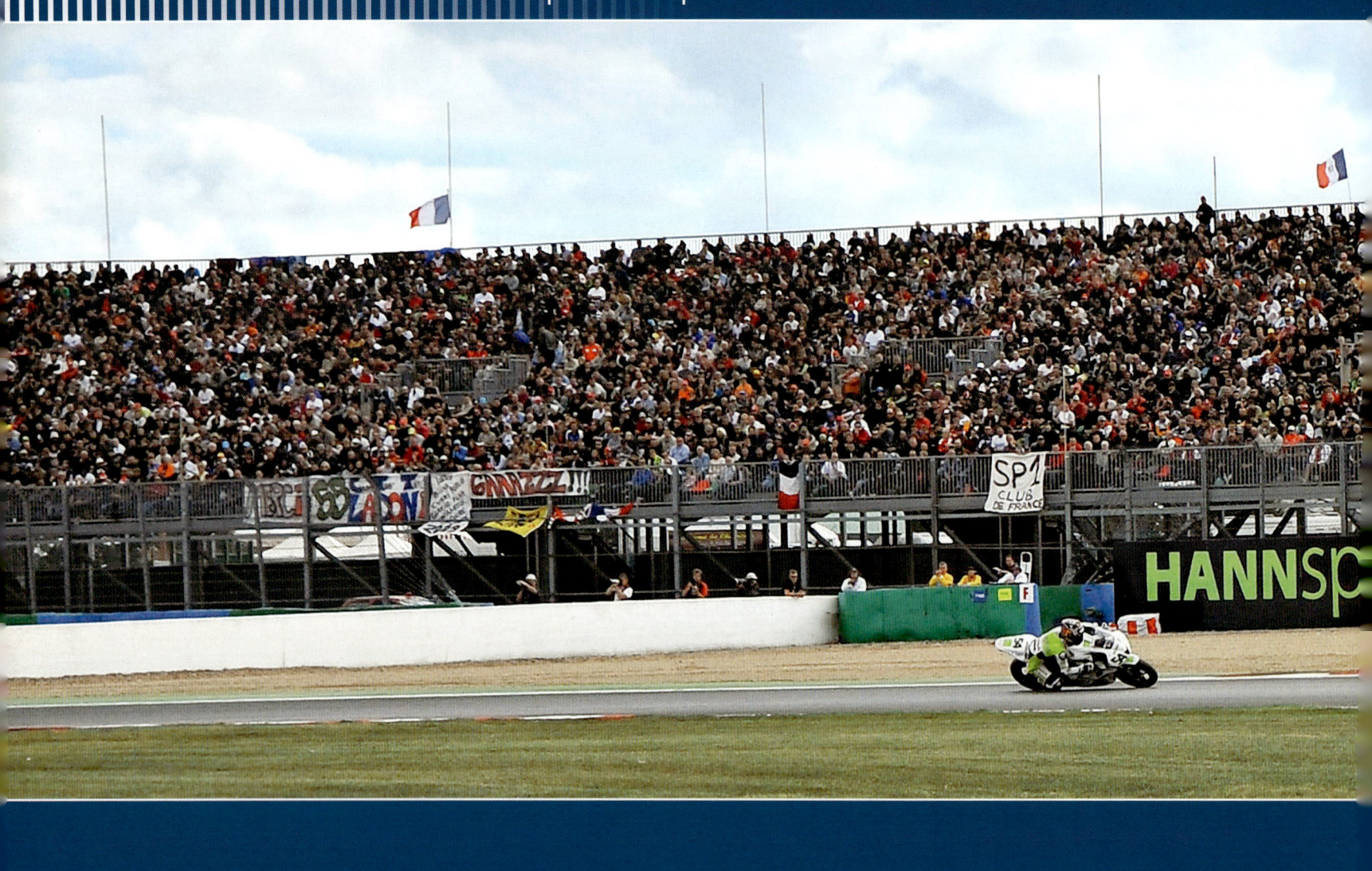

# SUPERSPORT RACES

## WSS Champion
# Cal Crutchlow

In his own words, Cal Crutchlow "came from the back streets of Coventry" to win the 2009 World Supersport Championship, a deserved overall victory that puts him into the record books as the first Yamaha rider since Jörg Teuchert in 2000 to take the title on the YZF-R6.

In the UK, the large city of Coventry is hardly synonymous with glamour and glitz. Nearby Birmingham is far better known outside the UK, and is also far bigger in terms of population.

Located the heartlands of the industrial midlands of England, Coventry has actually become a byword for an old saying, "He's been sent to Coventry." That means the person in question has been sent away in disgrace, shunned by his peer group.

The origins of the very peculiarly English saying are still being argued over even now, but there is nothing but pride in Coventry from its residents, and they have another thing to be proud of now, Cal Crutchlow, nicknamed 'The Dog', after his remarkable rookie season win. And nothing but pride from Crutchlow at being a product of Coventry. As it should be.

And you can bet people around the world will be paying attention should another top rider arrive on the scene with the place of birth and talent of Crutchlow.

At the start of the 2009 season few people would have put Cal down as a potential champion, particularly as he has spent the previous couple of BSB seasons on Superbike machinery; a Rizla Suzuki which gave him no wins and an HM Plant Honda that gave him only two. There were simply too many other good rider and bike combos around, much more experienced than Cal. Add to that the fact that the previous two world champions, Sofuoglu and Pitt, were riding for Ten Kate Honda, the team that had won all of the last seven WSS Rider's titles.

For Cal, they were just another two riders to beat.

Cal thinks that he is more of a natural Supersport rider than a Superbike rider, and the evidence that he would be good this year, even up in the top strata of global Su-

SPIDI
YAMAHA
YAMAHA
R6
DENSO
BECKER CARBON
YEC
YAMALUBE
PIRELLI
AKRAPOVIĆ
Pro-Bolt
Checkpoint
Beta

# WSS Champion

persport racing, was there for all to see. In 2004, he was tenth in the British Supersport series, in 2005 he was fourth, taking two wins and six podiums, but a year later he won it, on the same Northpoint Ekerold Honda machine, scoring six wins and beating - would you believe it - Eugene Laverty.

He cut his early racing teeth against the likes of Chaz Davies and Casey Stoner, in national one-make championships, and his grounding in racing was amplified by being chosen to run in the ACU Road Race Academy, designed to bring young riders to the fore.

He was also second in the Virgin Yamaha Cup, and all this one make racing, beating riders on identical machines, showed that more often than not Crutchlow was bringing a considerable degree of talent and determination to bear.

Racing is in the genes for Crutchlow, who was taken around the tracks of the UK and Europe by his ex-racer father, Derek. Strangely, for the young Crutchlow this was all not that interesting until the age of 11, when he started averaging two hours a day on an old dirtbike, and he was hooked

*Crutchlow had a great year, winning the Supersport title despite a couple of errors in his first full season in the category. The superiority of the Cal-Yamaha package was plain for all to see and the title confirmed it.*

# WSS Champion

*Crutchlow had several rivals in the title battle, including the surprise of the season Eugene Laverty (50), while Kenan Sofuoglu (54) was competitive again in the second half of the season on the Ten Kate Honda.*

on the racing drug from then on. He was also a talented football player but chose the option of racing, and now he should feel happy that he did.

For kicks, and training nowadays, Crutchlow is a keen cyclist, and only an hour or two after winning the world championship he was in pitlane at Portimao, meeting with British resident French rider Sylvain Guintoli, to arrange a new partnership for his long distance cycle rides in the English Midlands.

Born on October 29 1985, Crutchlow is already a world champion at 23, but ambition is ever resident in the fighting spirit of Crutchlow. With a top level Yamaha WSB machine, and a fellow Englishman James Toseland as a team-mate in 2010, he won't have to wait long to get to grips with a new class again after his glorious single season in WSS.

His WSB record is already impressive, having scored a podium as a wildcard in the UK last year (second at Donington) and qualified second on the grid at Portimao in 2008, when riding his BSB Honda.

Arai
MONSTER
BECKER CARBON
R6
DENSO
YAMAHA
YAMALUBE
PIRELLI
Pro-Bolt
AKRAPOVIC
BöCKERS
Checkpoint
gilles.tooling
Beta
TORNADO

# WSS
# Riders

From round 3 onwards Cal Crutchlow never relinquished the lead of the championship, while from round 4 onwards it was the turn of Eugene Laverty to firmly establish the second place slot as his own. Even though the Irishman had one eye on the title after Imola where Crutchlow crashed, the 23-year-old Parkalgar man also crashed out at Magny-Cours and that was the end of his hopes.

Laverty joined the Supersport championship trail half-way through the 2008 season after racing in 250 GP, and he was already a winner by the second round of this year in Qatar after taking his Parkalgar Honda CBR to the top slot. Eugene then stepped onto the top of the podium three more times during the year, winning at Assen, Kyalami and Portimao. At the end of the season only seven points separated him from Crutchlow: without his error in France, Laverty could surely have been in with a better chance of fighting for the title at the final round.

Three wins went to Kenan Sofuoglu, the 2007 World Supersport champion returning to this more congenial category, for him at least, following his disappointing experience in Superbike in 2008. The Turkish rider won the opening round at Phillip Island, but then had to wait until US Round to take another win, and this was followed by a third at Imola. Kenan looked pretty competitive in the first part of the season, despite a few problems with his Ten Kate Honda CBR600R, while in the second half he had two DNFs that kept him out of the title fight.

Spain's Joan Lascorz had a positive mid-season run, justifying his (and his Motocard.com team's) clamorous decision to switch from Honda to Kawasaki for this season. 24-year-old Lascorz turned out to be a true revelation, the Barcelona rider notching up one win at Magny-Cours and five podiums throughout the season.

Two former world champions were next up in fifth and sixth place with one win each to their name. 36-year-old Fabien Foret, 2002 champion, scored half the number of points of his Yamaha team-mate Crutchlow, while 33-year-old Andrew Pitt (2001 and 2008 champion) with the other Ten Kate Honda didn't fare any better.

And still on the subject of in-team clashes between experts and younger talent, Katsuaki Fujiwara also lost out to Lascorz in Kawasaki. The 34-year-old Japanese rider may continue to

Red Bull
SHOEI
autódromo internacional algarve
GALP motoAction
Portimão
Albufeira
aurora group
Radisson BLU RESORT, PORTIMAO
WWW.TRACK4APARTMENTS.COM
PIRELLI
HONDA
Dread
MoTeC
KING DICK TOOLS
EVOTECH
AKRAPOVIC
NGK SPARK PLUGS
ÖHLINS
alpinestars

have an excellent reputation as a test-rider, but he has not been seen in the top echelons of Supersport for some time now, despite being on a competitive machine.

Anthony West was probably distracted by his Stiggy team's financial difficulties, which forced him to miss the final round. The Australian began the season well but then lost his way somewhat, and only managed to get back onto the podium again at Brno. The former 250 GP rider was banking a lot on emerging this season, but in the end his form was conditioned by a series of problems.

There is one rider however at the age of 37 who continues to give the best of himself, even when it comes to accepting new challenges. We're talking about Garry McCoy, who took his Triumph onto the podium twice, and finished eighth overall. The three-cylinder British bike (run by the Italian ParkinGo BEI Racing team) did not have the same sort of development as the Japanese bikes but the veteran Australian gave his all and was almost always ahead of his team-mates, Gianluca Nannelli and then Chaz Davies.

When he didn't crash, another Australian Mark Aitchison also showed what he was capable of on the Althea Honda machine and he finished ninth overall. The 26-year-old from Gosford showed that the Italian team's CBR was competitive and maybe an increased focus on this class could have given greater satisfaction for the Rome-based team, which could also count on the services of Matthieu Lagrive before he was moved up to Superbike.

# WSS Riders

*Even though only Eugene Laverty (50) had a real chance of fighting for the title with Cal Crutchlow, Joan Lascorz (26) and Kenan Sofuoglu (54) were the other two protagonists of the 2009 Supersport World Championship season. More had been expected from Fabien Foret (99) and Andrew Pitt (1).*

# Supersport Races

# Phillip Island (AUS) (01.03)

The first pole position of the 2009 season was set by Kenan Sofuoglu, ahead of Lascorz and Pitt.

The race began with a terrific scrap between Pitt (Honda), Lascorz (Kawasaki), Crutchlow (Yamaha), Laverty (Honda), Aitchison (Honda), Veneman (Suzuki), Foret (Yamaha), West (Honda) and Sofuoglu (Honda), all in the space of a couple of seconds, while the others were not far behind.

At the mid-point, those in the leading group were also joined by Massimo Roccoli (Honda), Garry McCoy and Gianluca Nannelli (Triumph), but Sofuoglu and Pitt looked as if they were in control of proceedings, despite having to hold off the attacks from Anthony West (Honda), who was right on their exhausts.

On the final lap there were three Hondas in the space of a handkerchief, with the two Ten Kate men ganging up to shut out West. The Stiggy rider tried right until the flag, but Sofuoglu was the quickest on the track and the Turk took the chequered flag ahead of Pitt and West. Yamaha came off worst from the Australian race, Crutchlow taking fourth in a photo-finish in the middle of five Hondas, and over a second away from the leading trioe.

*Three Hondas on the podium in the opening round of the 2009 championship and a win for Kenan Sofuoglu (54) ahead of reigning champion Andrew Pitt (1).*

### Results

| | | | |
|---|---|---|---|
| 1° | K. Sofuoglu | (TUR - Honda) | 33'42"156 |
| | | | 166,180 km/h |
| 2° | A. Pitt | (AUS - Honda) | + 0"060 |
| 3° | A. West | (AUS - Honda) | + 0"153 |
| 4° | C. Crutchlow | (GBR - Yamaha) | + 1"097 |
| 5° | E. Laverty | (IRL - Honda) | + 1"098 |

# (14.03) Losail (QATAR)

*Eugene Laverty (50) appeared in the winners' circle for the first time by taking victory ahead of Pitt (1) and Crutchlow (35).*

Finally a new name appeared in the Supersport list of winners: Eugene Laverty. In his first full world championship season the 22 year-old from Toomebridge (Northern Ireland) scored a comprehensive win over the two Ten Kate Honda riders, Pitt and Sofuoglu, who tried to attack him in the final stages of the race. Laverty, who won on a Honda run by the Anglo-Portuguese Parkalgar team, had already shown what he was capable of in the 2008 Vallelunga race, when he scored a podium as stand-in rider for the injured Foret on the factory Yamaha.

Poleman Cal Crutchlow had a good race on the factory Yamaha R6 machine, the Coventry man taking on seven Hondas in the early stages after his team-mate Foret had crashed early on. Cal eventually picked up the final podium place amidst a sea of Honda machines.

More than five seconds behind could be found two more Hondas, the Veidec version of Harms and the Althea machine of Lagrive. The battle for fifth place also included Australian Mark Aitchison, but he crashed on lap 6, and then remounted to finish in 15th place.

After two rounds, the World Championship was headed by Pitt (Honda) on 40 points, ahead of Sofuoglu (Honda) on 38, Laverty (Honda) on 36 and Crutchlow (Yamaha) on 29.

## Results

| | | | |
|---|---|---|---|
| 1° | E. Laverty | (IRL - Honda) | 37'06"285 |
| | | | 156,595 km/h |
| 2° | A. Pitt | (AUS - Honda) | + 0"063 |
| 3° | C. Crutchlow | (GBR - Yamaha) | + 0"625 |
| 4° | K. Sofuoglu | (TUR - Honda) | + 0"711 |
| 5° | R. Harms | (DEN - Honda) | + 5"200 |

# Supersport Races

Arai
SPIDI
www.cia-insurance.co.uk
YAMAHA
R6
BECKER
CARBON
DENSO
35

# (05.04) Valencia (ESP)

After setting pole position in qualifying, Yamaha man Cal Crutchlow then went on to beat the Hondas, getting the better of Anthony West, the race leader until the final stages when he was passed by Cal. The rain that fell before the start forced the riders to risk in their choice of tyres, but the top men opted for the same solution because the weather looked as if it would improve. Michele Pirro (Yamaha) surprised everyone by taking the lead, but he was soon caught by the top men.

The Italian remained in the leading group, which was headed by Crutchlow (Yamaha) ahead of West (Honda), Sofuoglu (Honda), Lagrive (Honda), Aitchison (Honda) and Fuijwara (Kawasaki).

The first three pulled out a lead, while the rest were more than 20 seconds off the leader's pace.

Half-way through the leading group began to break up, with West and Crutchlow pulling away. At the flag it was the Yamaha man who took the win over the Australian. The Ten Kate Honda riders were struggling, Sofuoglu finishing third and Pitt down in thirteenth.

This result added weight to the rumours regarding the alleged technical infringement perpetrated by the Dutch team up until Qatar.

In the standings, Crutchlow and Sofuoglu were equal on top with 54 points, followed by a trio made up of West, Laverty and Pitt, all on 43.

*In his debut season in Supersport, Cal Crutchlow (35) gave Yamaha its first win of the year ahead of West (13) on a Honda.*

### Race 1

| | | | |
|---|---|---|---|
| 1° | C. Crutchlow | (GBR - Yamaha) | 38'15"613 |
| | | | 144,456 km/h |
| 2° | A. West | (AUS - Honda) | + 0"171 |
| 3° | K. Sofuoglu | (TUR - Honda) | + 8"408 |
| 4° | M. Aitchison | (AUS - Honda) | + 12"421 |
| 5° | K. Fuijwara | (JPN - Kawasaki) | + 16"529 |

# (26.04) Assen (NL)

*Three different manufacturers on the podium and a second win for Eugene Laverty (50), who came home ahead of Crutchlow (35, in front of Foret) and Lascorz (26).*

On the opening laps of the fourth round of the World Championship, the leading group was made up of Lascorz (Kawasaki), Laverty (Honda), Pitt (Honda) and Crutchlow (Yamaha). The Englishman had made a fantastic recovery from tenth place at the end of lap 1 following a poor start. Foret (Yamaha) then also joined the top 4 at the front.

A third of the way through the race, Joan Lascorz was leading but his rivals were right on his tail and the group was about to get bigger with the arrival of West, Sofuoglu, Aitchison and Harms, all on Hondas.

Lap 16 saw two surprises when Foret overshot and forced Crutchlow to brake; behind them Pitt tried to capitalize but he crashed out of the race.

At this point the battle for the win was between Laverty and Lascorz, while Crutchlow took third place ahead of Foret, Sofuoglu and Aitchison.

The final laps were thrilling, with three riders on three different machines fighting for teh win: Irishman Eugene Laverty on the Parkalgar Honda, Joan Lascorz of Spain with the increasingly rapid Kawasaki Motocard-com machine, and above all Cal Crutchlow on the factory Yamaha R6.

Cal pulled out all the stops with a couple of daring moves to stay behind the leading duo, but he didn't give up and was rewarded with a splendid second place after Laverty had taken Lascorz for the win.

## Results

| | | | |
|---|---|---|---|
| 1° | E. Laverty | (IRL - Honda) | 35'45"160 |
| | | | 160,528 km/h |
| 2° | C. Crutchlow | (GBR - Yamaha) | + 0"107 |
| 3° | J. Lascorz | (ESP - Kawasaki) | + 0"178 |
| 4° | F. Foret | (FRA - Yamaha) | + 1"777 |
| 5° | K. Sofuoglu | (TUR - Honda) | + 1"901 |

# Supersport Races

# Supersport Races

# (10.05) Monza (ITA)

**W**ith a top speed of 288 km/h, Cal Crutchlow set another pole position, ahead of Lascorz on the Kawasaki and Foret on the other Yamaha. The Supersport championship was now seeing the rise of other protagonists since the Ten Kate Honda team had had their electric fuel pump removed. Monza saw a second win for Cal Crutchlow on the Yamaha, the new Supersport star, and the Englishman got the better of Laverty (Honda) and Foret (Yamaha) to take the win by 2.5 seconds.

While Crutchlow was confirming his run of form, the same could also be said for Joan Lascorz, who despite being on a rather less competitive Kawasaki, pulled out all the stops to stay with Cal and then defended his second place from the attacks of Foret and Laverty.

Foret returned to the top ranks with a third place, and Laverty's fourth helped him to hold onto second place in the championship.

And in the standings, Crutchlow and Laverty led the way, followed by Sofuoglu, who was only ninth at Monza, Pitt, West (who crashed) and Lascorz.

*Two Yamahas on the podium in Italy with a win for Crutchlow ahead of Lascorz (26, in the photo ahead of Aitchison) and Foret (99).*

### Results

| | | | |
|---|---|---|---|
| 1° | C. Crutchlow | (GBR - Yamaha) | 29'34"605 |
| | | | 188,029 km/h |
| 2° | J. Lascorz | (ESP - Kawasaki) | + 2"660 |
| 3° | F. Foret | (FRA - Yamaha) | + 2"716 |
| 4° | E. Laverty | (IRL - Honda) | + 2"780 |
| 5° | A. Pitt | (AUS - Honda) | + 9"270 |

# (17.05) Kyalami (ZA)

*Another win for Laverty (50), who held off the much-feared Crutchlow (35). Aitchison (8) was third but some way behind.*

Three Hondas powered into the lead with Sofuoglu, Laverty and Pitt, who pulled out a gap to Lascorz (Kawasaki), while poleman Crutchlow was sixth, over two seconds behind. Eugene Laverty then took over at the front and in two laps gained almost two seconds on Pitt, Lascorz, Foret (Yamaha), Crutchlow (Yamaha) and Sofuoglu.

While Laverty was running a solo race in the lead, with an advantage of over four seconds, five riders were battling for the runner-up slot. On lap 6 however Cal Crutchlow pulled the pin and set off after his Irish rival, while the trailing group was joined by Aitchison (Honda). The gap between Laverty and Crutchlow remained wide at over three seconds, but this did not bring a halt to the charge of the Irishman, who took his lead over the next man Foret to over six seconds.

With a third of the race still to go, Crutchlow managed to reduce the gap to 2.5 seconds, but Laverty continued to control the situation. Foret was still third, while Sofuoglu and Lascorz also pulled away from the following group made up of Aitchison, Nannelli and Pitt. Foret crashed four laps from the end, but nothing else happened until the chequered flag, with Laverty running out the winner by over 1.5 seconds from Crutchlow, while Mark Aitchison put in a fantastic last lap to grab the final podium slot from Lascorz and Sofuoglu.

In the standings, Crutchlow was now leading on 119 points, with Laverty on 106 and Sofuoglu on 83.

## Results

| | | | |
|---|---|---|---|
| 1° | E. Laverty | (IRL - Honda) | 39'06''061 |
| | | | 149,855 km/h |
| 2° | C. Crutchlow | (GBR - Yamaha) | + 2''546 |
| 3° | M. Aitchison | (AUS - Honda) | + 17''358 |
| 4° | J. Lascorz | (ESP - Kawasaki) | + 17''454 |
| 5° | K. Sofuoglu | (TUR - Honda) | + 18''221 |

YAMAHA
Arai
35
DENSO
YAMAHA
YAMAHA
YAMAHA

HONDA
GENUINE ACCESSORIES
altec
PIRELLI
HONDA
sbs
FMA
altec

WSS Races

# (31•05) Miller (USA)

**E**ugene Laverty got the best start, shadowed by Crutchlow and Nannelli, who was passed after a few turns by poleman Lascorz. On the second lap, the Yamaha man forced his way past Laverty to take the lead, but it didn't last long because the Irishman immediately took over once again.

Garry McCoy was putting in a good run with the Triumph in fourth place, setting a new circuit record along the way.

On the seventh lap Melissa Paris crashed at turn 1, depriving the results sheet of the only female racer in this category.

The leading foursome, Laverty, Crutchlow, Lascorz and Sofuoglu, continued in single file, gradually pulling out a gap to the rest of the field.

It looked as if Crutchlow and Laverty were going right down to the wire for the win, but two laps from the end Sofuoglu was right with the leading duo, while Cal tried in turn to take the lead as he could see that Laverty was struggling a bit.

The last lap was a real thriller, with Kenan Sofuoglu getting in between the two leaders and after barging his way past Crutchlow, overtook Laverty to go on and take his second win of the year, while at the same time restoring some credibility to the team.

In the championship, Crutchlow was leading with 135 points, ahead of Laverty with 126 and Sofuoglu, who was back in the hunt on 108.

*Kenan Sofuoglu (54) took the win again but all attention was focussed on the two women on the starting-grid, Melissa Paris (29) and Marie-Josè Boucher (38).*

### Results

| | | | |
|---|---|---|---|
| 1° | K. Sofuoglu | (TUR - Honda) | 34'00"510 |
| | | | 155,831 km/h |
| 2° | E. Laverty | (IRL - Honda) | + 0"368 |
| 3° | C. Crutchlow | (GBR - Yamaha) | + 0"521 |
| 4° | J. Lascorz | (ESP - Kawasaki) | + 1"833 |
| 5° | F. Foret | (FRA - Yamaha) | + 12"071 |

# (21·06) Misano (RSM)

*In the battle between Crutchlow (35) and Laverty (50), the win went to the Coventry man, while Massimo Roccoli stepped onto the podium.*

Misano saw a third win of the season come the way of Cal Crutchlow, in a race that was restarted after the red flags had come out.

In the first part Massimo Roccoli took the lead, but Pitt passed him before crashing out on lap 3, all of which left Laverty in charge. Poleman Michele Pirro got off to a bad start but by the end of lap 4 was in eighth place but running at the same pace as the leaders. Crutchlow then set a new lap record to catch Laverty on lap 6.

A third of the way through the race, Sofuoglu crashed and Pirro also ended up on the ground in an attempt to avoid him.

The red flags were waved and the race was interrupted.

In the second part Crutchlow immediately powered into the lead, followed by Lascorz, while Laverty and Roccoli trailed a short distance behind. Just over half-way through and Crutchlow was still in the lead, but now ahead of Laverty, Lascorz and Roccoli, but in the aggregate standings it was Laverty up at the front.

On the last lap the Yamaha man took the lead, Laverty tried in vain to surprise him in a sprint finish to the line, but Crutchlow won to consolidate his championship lead, 160 points against 146 for Laverty.

There was a funny epilogue to the race as the top two shook hands to celebrate, Laverty lost control of his bike and touched Crutchlow; the latter managed to stay upright, while Laverty crashed, without any serious consequences!

## Aggregate Results

| | | | |
|---|---|---|---|
| 1° | C. Crutchlow | (GBR - Yamaha) | 36'51"032 |
| | | | 151,377 km/h |
| 2° | E. Laverty | (IRL - Honda) | + 0"263 |
| 3° | M. Roccoli | (ITA - Honda) | + 16"289 |
| 4° | J. Lascorz | (ESP - Kawasaki) | + 20"894 |
| 5° | M. Aitchison | (AUS - Honda) | + 21"615 |

WSS Races

161

# Supersport Races

# Donington (GBR) (28.06)

Lascorz powered into the lead at the start, shadowed by Crutchlow (polesitter once again!) and Laverty, while Sofuoglu immediately lost touch and had to deal with Aitchison, McCoy and Fuijwara. On lap 3 Laverty crashed but his bike remained in the middle of the track while the field swarmed around it luckily without any problems; Laverty restarted from last place. In the meantime Crutchlow had passed Lascorz and was now in the lead. Another crash on lap 4 involved Fuijwara, who crashed into Aitichison while they were fighting for fourth place.

A third of the way through Crutchlow and Lascorz were running together for the lead, followed by Sofuoglu more than 1.5 seconds behind. McCoy was fourth, two seconds behind the Turkish rider but more than six seconds ahead of Foret.

At the mid-point, McCoy made a nice overtaking move on Sofuoglu to take third, while Laverty was on a charge and had moved up to eighth, and was now challenging for sixth in the group made up of Vizziello, Veneman, Laverty, Pitt, Nannelli and Dell'Omo.

A painful ankle, which he had picked up in qualifying, failed to slow Cal Crutchlow, who put the hammers down and headed for his fourth win of the year.

Behind finished Lascorz, the only rider able to challenge him, while Garry McCoy gave Triumph its first ever podium in the Supersport category.

The table now saw Crutchlow firmly in charge with 185 points, followed by Laverty on 157 and Sofuoglu on 121.

*Another win for Cal Crutchlow (35) who was now pulling ahead in the world championship. Behind him finished Lascorz and the surprising Triumph with Garry McCoy (24).*

## Results

| | | | |
|---|---|---|---|
| 1° | C. Crutchlow | (GBR - Yamaha) | 34'15"876 |
| | | | 154,981 km/h |
| 2° | J. Lascorz | (ESP - Kawasaki) | + 5"391 |
| 3° | G. McCoy | (AUS - T. Daytona 675) | + 14"918 |
| 4° | K. Sofuoglu | (TUR - Honda) | + 22"248 |
| 5° | E. Laverty | (IRL - Honda) | + 37"054 |

# (26.07) Brno (Czech Rep.)

*A major upset came in the Czech Republic with the retirement of Crutchlow (35), who left the win to Foret (99) in a sprint finish from West (13) and Lascorz (26).*

It was no surprise to see Crutchlow pick up yet another pole position in qualifying, ahead of Laverty and Lascorz.

The British rider led the race from lap 2 onwards after taking over at the front from Lascorz, and he appeared to be on his way to an easy fifth win of the season when his Yamaha inexplicably rolled to a halt two laps from the end.

Team-mate Fabien Foret took over at the front and went on to win on a circuit where the previous year his career had almost been ended following a nasty crash in qualifying. The Yamaha man capitalized on a drop in performance by Joan Lascorz at the end, the Spaniard finishing in third place after being passed by Anthony West. The Australian together with Fujiwara finished behind Foret, with the top 4 split by four-tenths at the flag. South African Morais had a positive debut in the category, finishing in sixth place but some way behind the leaders.

In the championship table Crutchlow was still at the top with 185 points, 17 more than Laverty, who had closed up the gap following Crutchlow's DNF, despite only finishing fifth. Third was Sofuoglu, who could only finish ninth at Brno, 57 points behind the leader.

## Results

| | | | |
|---|---|---|---|
| 1° | F. Foret | (FRA - Yamaha) | 37'14"367 |
| | | | 156,695 km/h |
| 2° | A. West | (AUS - Honda) | + 0"148 |
| 3° | J. Lascorz | (ESP - Kawasaki) | + 0"289 |
| 4° | K. Fujiwara | (JPN - Kawasaki) | + 0"400 |
| 5° | E. Laverty | (IRL - Honda) | + 6"823 |

# Supersport Races

# Supersport Races

# Nürburgring (GER) (06.09)

In the only qualifying session Crutchlow set a time that left the others standing. Second place man, the former World Supersport champion Kenan Sofuoglu was a full 1.4 seconds behind, while his chief rival for the title, Eugene Laverty, started from third on the grid.
In the race the Yamaha man powered away into the lead followed by Kenan Sofuoglu but at the end of lap 1 the Turkish rider was already half a second down. Behind the leading pair Lascorz and Laverty were fighting for third place. On lap 6 Sofuoglu crashed and then remounted but he was clearly out of the battle for the win.

The fight for the runner-up slot was now between Laverty and Lascorz, but they were a full ten seconds adrift...
Roccoli was running a lonely race in fourth while there was a terrific scrap for fifth between Foret, Aitchison and Harms. Nothing else happened until the flag and Crutchlow took the win from Laverty, who won a great battle with Lascorz.
With three rounds left, the table now saw Crutchlow increase his lead over Laverty to 22 points, while Sofuoglu remained on 128 and was virtually out of the title battle, 62 points behind the leader.

*rutchlow was back to his winning ways again in Germany, the Yamaha man finishing way ahead of Laverty (50) and Lascorz (26), while Roccoli (55) took fourth place.*

## Results

| | | | |
|---|---|---|---|
| 1° | C. Crutchlow | (GBR - Yamaha) | 37'56''481 |
| | | | 154,348 km/h |
| 2° | E. Laverty | (IRL - Honda) | + 10''109 |
| 3° | J. Lascorz | (ESP - Kawasaki) | + 10''250 |
| 4° | M. Roccoli | (ITA - Honda) | + 31''980 |
| 5° | F. Foret | (FRA - Yamaha) | + 34''575 |

# (27.09) Imola (ITA)

*Crutchlow's crash not only left victory in the hands of Sofuoglu (54) but also allowed Laverty (50) to close up on the Yamaha man in the points table. Fabien Foret also finished on the podium.*

### Results

| | | | |
|---|---|---|---|
| 1° | K. Sofuoglu | (TUR - Honda) | 35'51"342 |
| | | | 156,936 km/h |
| 2° | E. Laverty | (IRL - Honda) | + 5"372 |
| 3° | F. Foret | (FRA - Yamaha) | + 6"450 |
| 4° | C. Davies | (GBR - Triumph) | + 15"847 |
| 5° | G. McCoy | (AUS - Triumph) | + 15"944 |

Cal Crutchlow took his ninth pole position in ten races, relegating Sofuoglu to second place. Lascorz was third quickest ahead of Roccoli.

Kenan Sofuoglu led the first lap, followed closely by Roccoli and Lascorz while Crutchlow was slightly down in fourth.

A third of the way through Sofuoglu and Lascorz were then in the lead, but they had Crutchlow right behind them.

At the mid-point the leading group pulled the pin, and there were numerous changes in position until lap 11 when Lascorz's Kawasaki began to smoke badly. Unfortunately the oil left on the track by the Spanish rider's bike forced the Race Direction to stop the race to clean the track up.

Laverty then led the field in the early stages of the second part, followed by Sofuoglu, Crutchlow and McCoy. Once again there was a three-way battle, this time though between Sofuoglu, Crutchlow and Laverty. Half-way through the second part Sofuoglu tried to pull away but Crutchlow was on him and successfully passed the Turkish rider to move into the lead.

Three laps from the end Crutchlow unbelievably crashed, leaving the win to Sofuoglu, who had just under a two second lead over Laverty. The scrap for third was also an exciting one, and the final podium slot went to Foret (also on aggregate), while Supersport rookie Davies with the Triumph finished fourth overall.

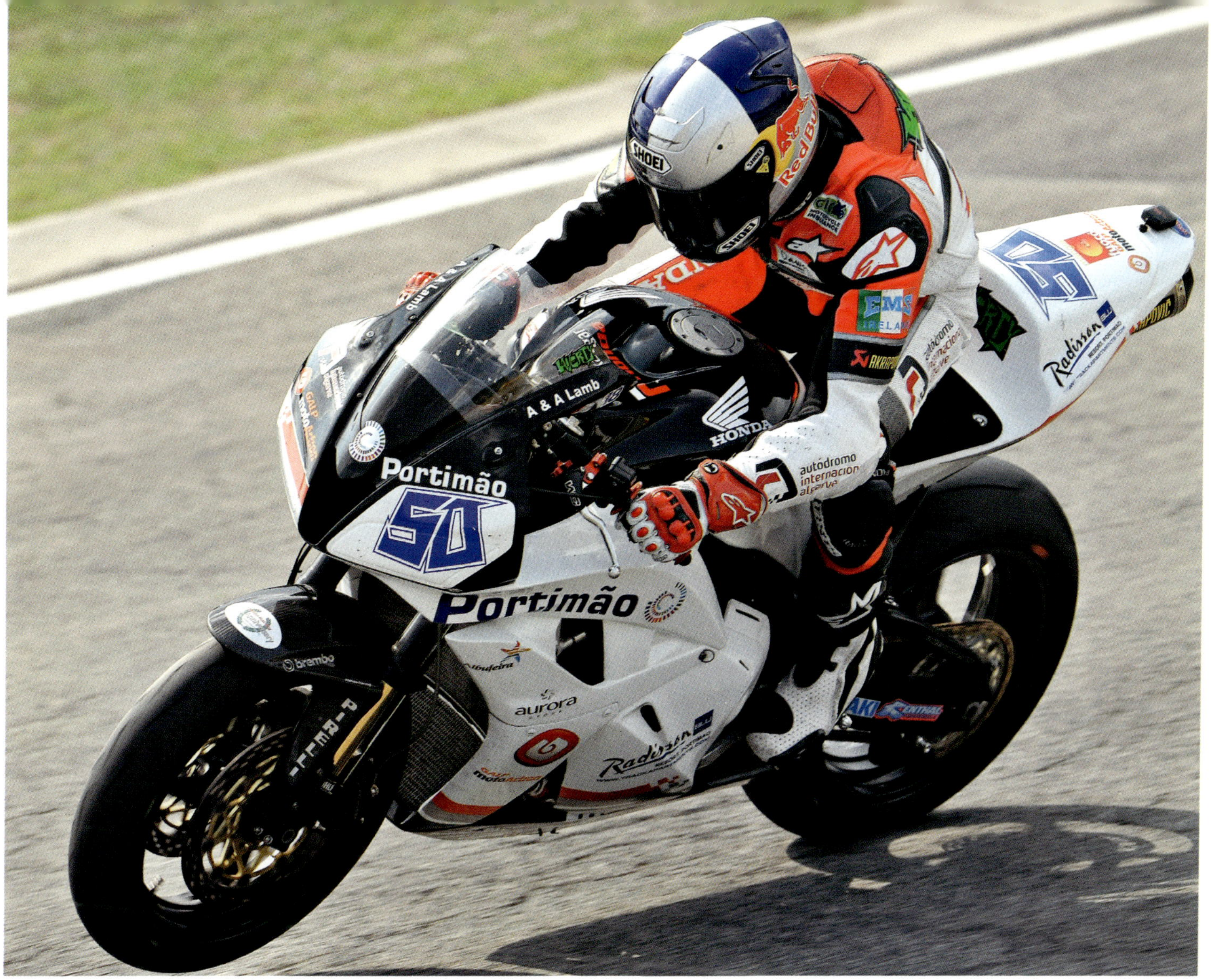

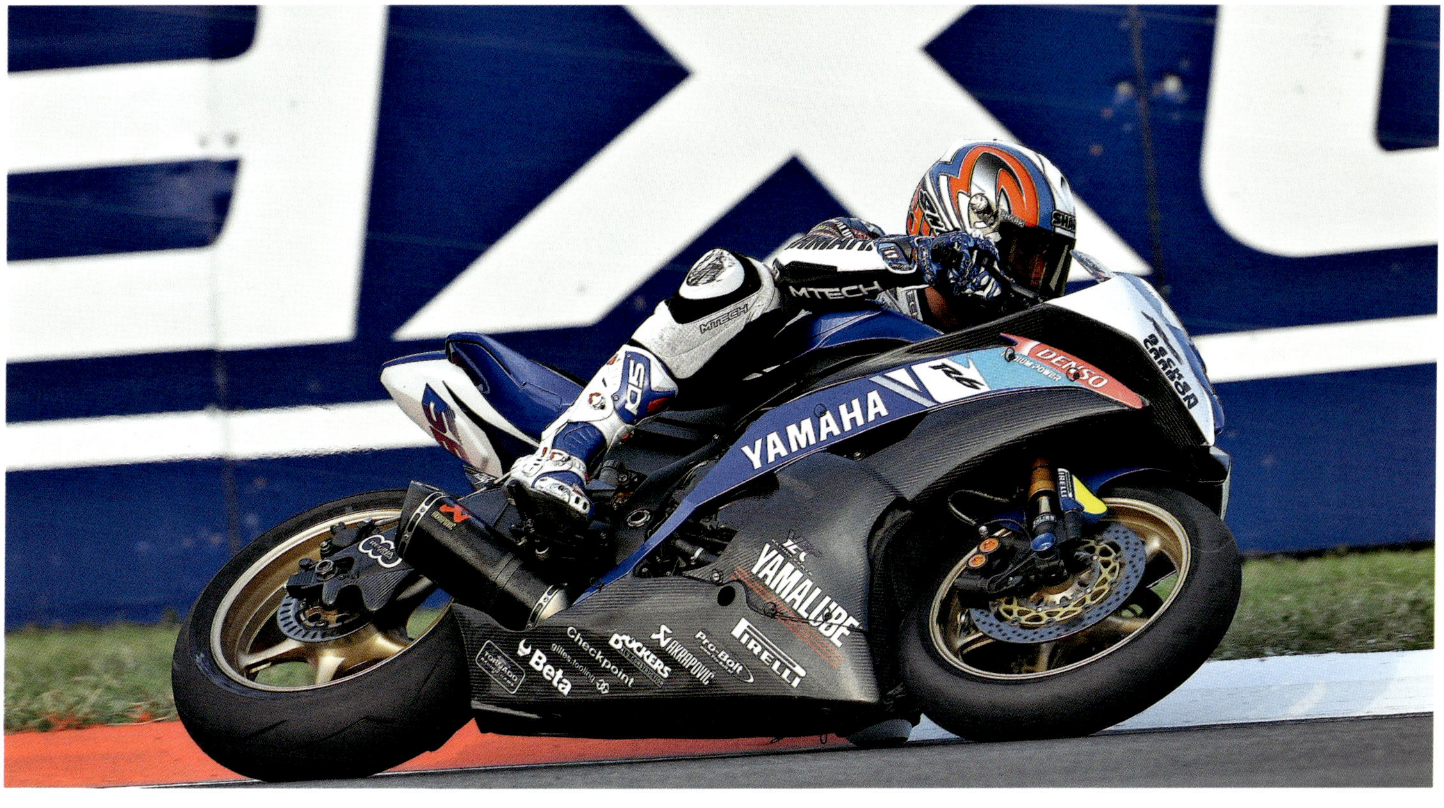

WSS Races

# (04.10)
# Magny Cours (FRA)

Cal Crutchlow powered to a new track record in qualifying ahead of Lascorz and Sofuoglu. The front row was completed by Laverty, the only rider still in with a chance of taking the title away from Crutchlow. Lascorz got a superb start and tried to pull away while Crutchlow came in hard on Laverty so as not to lose track of the Spaniard. The superior top speed of the R6 allowed Crutchlow to take control up front but neither Lascorz nor Laverty were giving up and Kawasaki's Spanish rider passed Cal on lap 3, immediately followed by the Irishman. At the end of lap 5 Joan Lascorz was still in the lead followed by Crutchlow, Laverty and Sofuoglu. Behind the leaders could be found another group headed by Aitchison and made up of Pitt, Fujiwara and West.

Half-way through Kenan Sofuoglu had latched on to the leading trio, which still had Lascorz as leader but the Kawasaki man was under pressure from Crutchlow and Laverty under braking. Unfortunately on lap 12 the Parkalgar man gave too much gas after taking Crutchlow and crashed out; he remounted but was too far away to make much of an impact. With a third of the race still to go Lascorz had a lead of almost two seconds over Crutchlow and as Laverty was some way behind Cal could settle for the second place that would bring him closer to the title. In the final stages the points leader upped his pace to try and go after Lascorz, while Sofuoglu rolled off and settled for third place. Two laps from the end the red flags came out for the presence of oil on the track.

The table now saw Crutchlow in the lead with 20 points over Laverty, and Sofuoglu in third.

*Once again the podium had three different manufacturers present: Kawasaki, Yamaha and Honda. The race was a hard-fought one with Lascorz (26) and Crutchlow (35) as protagonists while Laverty (50) crashed out and lost touch with the championship leader.*

## Results

| | | | |
|---|---|---|---|
| 1° | J. Lascorz | (ESP - Kawasaki) | 32'21"660 |
| | | | 155,389 km/h |
| 2° | C. Crutchlow | (GBR - Yamaha) | + 0"937 |
| 3° | K. Sofuoglu | (TUR - Honda) | + 5"910 |
| 4° | A. West | (AUS - Honda) | + 20"797 |
| 5° | M. Aitchison | (AUS - Honda) | + 20"992 |

# (25.10) Portimão (POR)

*The win by Eugene Laverty (50) in Portugal did not help the Irishman to take the title from Cal Crutchlow, who only needed a fourth place to be crowned champion. Kenan Sofuoglu (54) again proved himself to be a Supersport specialist, finishing runner-up at Portimao and third in the table. The podium was completed by Garry McCoy (24) with the Triumph.*

### Results

| | | | |
|---|---|---|---|
| 1. | E. Laverty | (IRL - Honda) | 35'17"044 |
| | | | 156,173 km/h |
| 2. | K. Sofuoglu | (TUR - Honda) | + 3"443 |
| 3. | G. McCoy | (AUS - Triumph) | + 13"874 |
| 4. | C. Crutchlow | (GBR - Yamaha) | + 15"144 |
| 5. | M. Aitchison | (AUS - Honda) | + 16"608 |

A rather unexciting race brought to an end an exciting season-long battle for the Supersport World Championship title, which went to Cal Crutchlow. The Coventry man put an end to years of Honda domination and brought back to Yamaha the riders' title for the first time in nine years (the last time was in 2009 with Teuchert).

The race win went to Eugene Laverty, who gave Honda their umpteenth Manufacturers' title, ahead of Kenan Sofuoglu. A Triumph completed the podium with Garry McCoy on board, a rider who despite his age continues to produce some excellent performances.

At the start Laverty tried to break away and on lap 1 already held a one second lead over Sofuoglu, Lascorz, Crutchlow, McCoy and Pirro. The Irishman then managed to gain a couple of seconds advantage over Sofuoglu, who after Joan Lascorz had retired with mechanical problems, had a second and a half lead over Crutchlow. The Yamaha man was in the meantime having to hold off McCoy, who was aiming for the podium and who on lap 9 passed Cal for third place. At the race's mid-point Laverty had a four and a half second lead over Sofuoglu.

At the chequered flag the win went to Laverty, but it failed to change the outcome of the title race. The Parkalgar man had more than three seconds lead over Sofuoglu and more than thirteen over McCoy. With fourth place, the 2009 title belonged to Crutchlow.

Sofuoglu, Lascorz and Foret finished behind Crutchlow and Laverty in the points in that order.

WSS Races

# STK 1000 Cup

# SUPERSTOCK RACES

# STK 1000 Champion
# Xavier Simeon

Following his European Superstock 600 title in 2006 and two years' experience in Superstock 1000, Xavier Simeon started the season as championship favourite. In addition, in 2009 the 20-year-old from Brussels was riding for the Ducati Xerox Junior Team (the winner the previous two years with Canepa and Roberts), and throughout the season he was on the 1098, the best performing machine on the grid.

The Simeon-Ducati winning package succeeded in taking the title thanks to ten podiums in ten races, which included five wins and five second places. "In this year's Superstock 1000 championship the lap times remained the same, but the level of the riders was lower than before", Simeon pointed out. "At the end of 2008 many of my rivals left the category and their places were taken by young inexperienced riders, who had to go through the learning curve. With one season behind them I am sure that next year we'll see a hard-fought category full of riders capable of challenging for the top positions."

Simeon's declared aim at the start of the year was to finish on the podium in every race; a result he achieved in full, and thanks to these consistent results he was able to take the title with one round remaining. "Only Berger and Corti were on the same level as me… and they were my main rivals throughout the season."

The year started off well with four second places in the first four rounds; a good result for the standings but not for Xavier's morale. "After Misano I started to question my form and decided that it was time to win races. Me and my team don't just turn up to go racing every weekend. We have the structure to win, and that was what we were supposed to be doing. From Donington onwards therefore, the music started to change …"

Simeon immediately found a good rapport in the squad run by Serafino Foti and the right feeling was created right from the start; he considers this to be one of the strong points of his season. "It's a well run-in team and it has the right experience to win. In the pit garages the guys are always having fun because they are passionate about their job but at the same time they are always very professional. Regarding the bike, the engine is one of the strong points of the Ducati 1098, the frame is not the best in the category but it's the perfect balance that makes all the difference."

STK 1000 Champion

# Superstock 1000 Champion

Analyzing Simeon's curriculum, with two Superstock titles to his name, the question begs as to whether or not a Superbike ride is the next step in his career. "I'm only 20 years of age", replied Xavier, who goes running and trains on a mountain-bike when he's not racing. "I'm still very young and I don't think I have the required experience to face up to Superbike in the best way possible. There, if you make a mistake that costs you three-tenths of a second, you lose 10 places. It's really tough …"
Furthermore Simeon wants his eventual move into the top class to be in a official team. The Belgian rider reckons the organizers should help to create a project dedicated to riders who win the Superstock classes, a project that would lead to a learning year with a factory team in Superbike. "It's no use making your debut in a new category with a team and a bike that you don't know, and use tyres you've never lapped with before. By the time you start to understand something the season is already over. A private team cannot afford that, whereas if you are a number 2 rider in a factory team, it's different".
Simeon is not really attracted by the Supersport category, and for this reason he sees his future in Superbike, Moto2 or MotoGP, with a clear aim in his head: to become World Champion.

*Xavier Simeon in action: his style is very 'clean' and he has looked good both on the four-cylinder Suzuki he raced until last year and the Ducati twin he was on in 2009. The Belgian had an excellent feeling with the Italian squad which also contributed to him taking the FIM Superstock 1000 Cup with one round remaining.*

# STK 1000 Riders

Five wins for Xavier Simeon, the winner of the FIM Superstock 1000 Cup, is the result that sums up this year's championship battle, but in the early part of the season it was Claudio Corti who led the way following wins at Valencia and Monza. Then from Misano onwards consistent results by the Belgian rider began to pay off, allowing Simeon to go on to take the crown.

Despite three second places the Suzuki Alstare man was unable to challenge the leader and the Italian had to settle for the runner-up slot. This was small satisfaction for a rider of the calibre of Corti who has raced in Superstock 1000 for a number of years, winning eight races and twice finishing runner-up in 2006 and 2007. But on the track the Japanese four-cylinder machine was unable to do much about the Ducati 1098R which once again proved to be the king of the category following its win in 2008.

The Suzuki was not the only bike to take second-best to the Italian twin-cylinder machine this year. The same could be said for the Honda CBR1000RR, the Kawasaki ZX10R and even the Yamaha R1, which were simply not in a position to maintain the pace of the Ducati, thus forcing their riders to scrap over the crumbs.

The third podium slot went to Maxime Berger, the 2007 European Superstock 600 champion, who despite winning three races had to take third best to Simeon and Corti in his second Superstock 1000 season (after finishing runner-up last year). The 20-year-old from Dijon proved to be so capable of riding the powerful Ten Kate Honda bike that at the end of the season his team gave him the chance to test a Superbike.

Not far behind Berger was one of the surprises of the season, Spain's Javier Fores, who finished on the podium four times despite having a rather unfancied bike in the shape of the Pedercini-prepared and run Kawasaki ZX10-R. Fores also scored points in the races, a demonstration of his true qualities. One of the season rookies, Daniele Beretta, also managed to score points in every race up until the final Portimao round. Unfortunately the Ducati Xerox Junior Team rider crashed out but he still managed to finish in sixth place, an important result in his first season

STK 1000 Riders

# STK 1000 Riders

Claudio Corti (Suzuki, previous page) was runner-up in Superstock 1000, the Italian finishing ahead of Maxime Berger (21, Honda), Javier Fores (12, Kawasaki), Sylvain Barrier (20, Yamaha) and Daniele Beretta (29, Ducati).

with such a difficult bike as the 1098R and in such a competitive category.

Beretta finished in the standings behind Sylvain Barrier, the best rider on a Yamaha R1 machine, which this year was not able to confirm itself at the top of the category. The 21-year-old Frenchman was always up at the front but was sidelined by a series of crashes. Sylvain eventually finished in fifth place. Another Frenchman, Loris Baz, the 16-year-old European Superstock 600 champion, managed to emerge on several occasions with a Yamaha R1 in his rookie 1000 season, finishing in the top 10.

A similar result was also achieved by Ondrej Cezek, one of the few riders from Eastern Europe capable of staying with the frontrunners. The young rider from Brno in the Czech Republic (he lives a short distance from the circuit) came up through minimotos and after racing in 600, this year joined the 1000 trail with an MS Racing Honda CBR1000RR.

The top 10 in the 2009 FIM Cup was completed by Austria's Renè Mahr, who after racing a KTM in 2008 switched to a TKR Suzuki this year, ending the season well; and Davide Giugliano, who is considered by many observers to be a real talent, but who still has to mature as a competitive rider. The 20-year-old from Rome, Italy began the season with an MV Agusta but then switched to a Suzuki and finished on a Yamaha.

# STK 600 Championship

# STK 600 RACES

STK 600 Champion

# STK 600 Champion
# Gino Rea

Leaning on the wall that divides the pit-lane from the track, Gino Rea observes as his number 4 Honda is wheeled into place alongside the Yamahas of Ben Spies and Cal Crutchlow for the traditional end-of-season 2009 championship-winning photo-shoot. When they call him for the group photo, he timidly approaches his SBK and Supersport counterparts, almost as if he does not consider himself worthy to be in their company. For this Englishman of Italian descent however, the Superstock 600 title is just a starting-point for further success.

"My dream is the same as everyone else's - to win a world championship in Superbike or MotoGP" he says.

The 20-year-old shows remarkable determination, that very same determination that took him to the European Superstock 600 title at the end of a positive season that began not without some difficulty.

"Unlike some of the other guys", said the newly-crowned champion, "I arrived at Valencia without having done any pre-season testing but the Ten Kate Honda Racing team did a great job to help me to become competitive". Rea was up against 30 or so riders in all ten of the scheduled rounds in the championship. And he won at the final race, when nerves of steel and a cool head were required. "Bussolotti, Lonbois and Petrucci were the riders to beat. It was hard because they started the season well and I needed to be consistent to beat them, but in the end I did it".

His rivals had to take second-best to the London rider's consistency and amazing recovery throughout the season, but Rea actually only realized he could win the European title before the last round at Portimao.

"I was aiming to do a good season at the top and I really hoped to be able to fight for the title but I only realized I could win it at the final round in Portugal."

It was a really tough race because four riders were in with a chance of taking the title, but at the flag the winner was Rea and his Ten Kate Honda team.

"They're a great team. We had a good relationship and it's also thanks to them that I won the

# STK 600 Champion

*Gino Rea celebrates after winning the European title at the Portimao circuit in Portugal. Despite finishing third, the British rider won the title by one point from Bussolotti.*

title. Now I can start thinking about the future. I'm going to stand outside Gerrit Ten Kate's office and beg for a Supersport ride!", jokes Gino as he looks towards the Dutch team's garage. "Winning the 600 title and then moving up to Supersport would be perfect and doing it with a team of this level would mean realizing a dream". So, as he waits for the phone to ring, Gino will be back out training on a motocross bike (an early passion of Rea's, as he was on a Honda QR bike at just three years of age) and on a mountain-bike.

But first, he would like to mention all the people who helped him to the European title: "I want to thank my team and Honda, also my dad and all my family, Andy Stone and my personal sponsors for backing me in this fantastic victory".

Arai
DAMEN LEATHERS
ids
TOYOTA
INDUSTRIAL EQUIPMENT
4
WWW.GEORGEWHITE.CO.UK
George WHITE
BT
PIRELLI
RACE

# STK 600 Riders

The battle for the European Superstock 600 title was only decided at the final round in Portugal, and the difference between first and fourth place after ten rounds, was just eight points.

This was a clear demonstration that the championship is a well-balanced one, full of riders under 20 years of age who obviously make up the talent breeding-ground for World Superbike and four-stroke racing in general.

As well as Gino Rea, the European champion and subject of the previous pages, it is worth mentioning at least three other riders who were the protagonists of the season, to which can be added a further three outsiders.

Next up in the standings was Marco Bussolotti, the 19 year-old from Ancona who after a chaotic start to the season (he unwittingly took out his team-mate Petrucci at Assen), from Misano Adriatico onwards was always up at the front, stepping onto the podium six times and winning at Donington and Portimao. The Yamaha Trasimeno rider lost the title by just one point from Rea, taking the runner-up slot for the second year in a row.

Vincent Lonbois is also 19 years of age but one of the veterans of the category, having made his debut in Superstock 600 at the end of 2006, but he had never come so close to winning the title (in 2008 he was eighth). The Belgian was fast but impetuous on occasions and his determined riding style offered a few 'hairy' moments. He won at Brno and at the Nurburgring while on four other occasions stepped onto the podium with the MTM Racing Yamaha.

Considered to be one of the brightest young Italian talents, Danilo Petrucci missed out on a chance to win the European title at the age of 19. He was the only rider to win three races but even considering his misfortune at Assen (and the contact with Lonbois at Donington), the rider from Terni lost his way in the final part of the season and then crashed out at Magny-Cours. Surely the Yamaha Italia Junior-Trasimeno team rider will go on to make amends in the future.

And still on the subject of Italian riders, 20 year-old Eddi La Marra finally had a good

STK 600 Riders

191

# STK 600 Riders

*Marco Bussolotti (previous page) lost the title to Rea by one point, while Vincent Lonbois (55) and Danilo Petrucci (9) were close behind. Eddi La Marra (47) of Italy and Florian Marino (21) of France scored one win apiece.*

season with the Lorini Honda team. The young Italian was up there in nearly all the races and after winning the first one of his career at Imola with a superb pass on Rea, Bussolotti and Petrucci at the Variante Bassa he scored his first pole position at Portimao. If he manages to keep things under control, he will surely be a rider to watch in the future, maybe in Superstock 1000.

Over the Alps meanwhile and the best French rider was 16 year-old Jeremy Guarnoni who, despite his age, is in his third season in the category. Guarnoni was in evidence particularly in the first part of the season, when he stepped onto the podium three times, but lost his way a bit in the second half, when he scored relatively few points.

Another French rider, this time making his debut in the series, was Florian Marino, who came from the 125 Rookie Cup and the French 600 Pirelli Junior Cup. Marino only took part in the last three races of the season, but had the satisfaction of winning the Magny-Cours round, beating all the top riders in the category.

SPYKE
CELESTINI
motostore
TERNANA SOCCORSO
Autocar
Candelori Mario
Conti
GS car
ERREBI
YAMAHA
SIMA
FIPEM
BONDINI
PIRELLI
bitubo
BEL-RAY
ARROW
FILCOMP CARENATURE
gpcrono

47
SINETICA

ELITE
HONDA
PIRELLI

Printed by
Grafiche Flaminia - Foligno (PG)
November 2009